Classic British Motorcycles

An Illustrated History

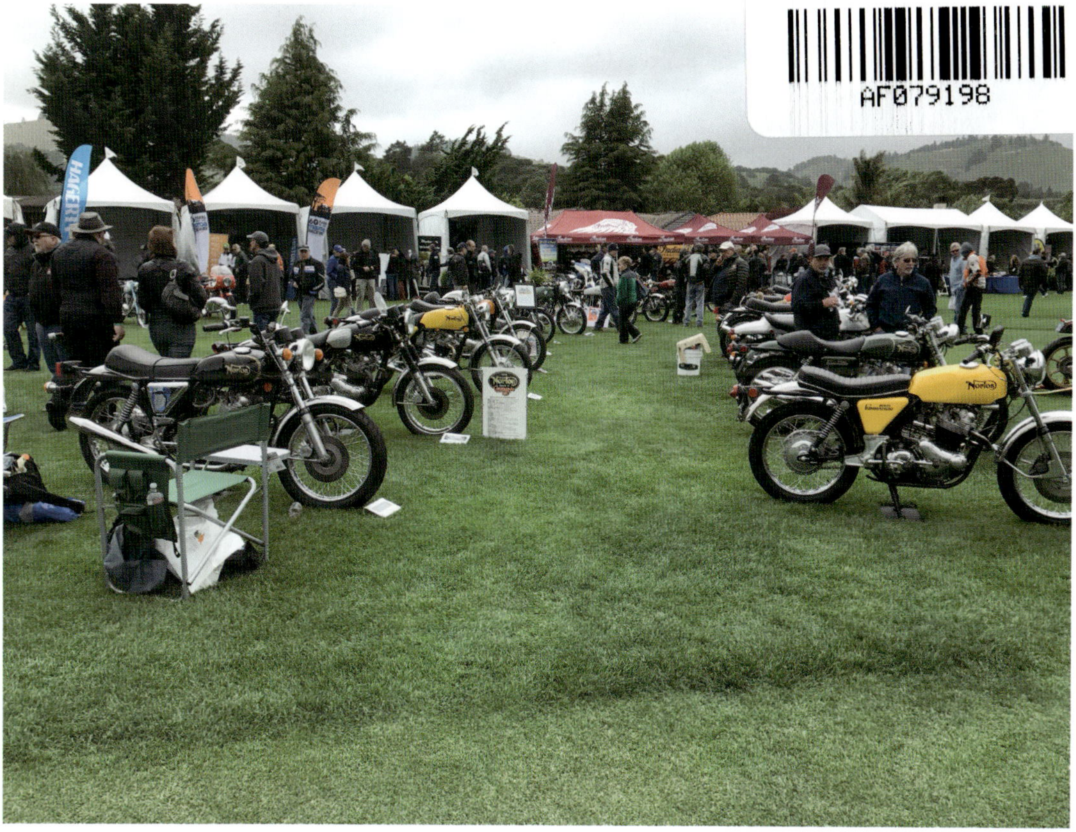

Andy Tallone

KEY Books

CLASSIC VEHICLES SERIES, VOLUME 4

Front cover image: The 1973 Triumph X-75 Hurricane began life as a BSA. However, BSA folded before it was ready, and Triumph inherited the project, which is why the motorcycles have BSA engines and frames. Sadly, barely 1,000 of these stunning machines were built.

Back cover image: This 1948 Matchless G80 typifies the classic post-war British motorcycle: undersquare 500cc OHV single, rigid frame, telescopic forks and loads of style.

Published by Key Books
An imprint of Key Publishing Ltd
PO Box 100
Stamford
Lincs PE19 1XQ

www.keypublishing.com

The right of Andy Tallone to be identified as the author of this book has been asserted in accordance with the Copyright, Designs and Patents Act 1988 Sections 77 and 78.

Copyright © Andy Tallone, 2021

ISBN 978 1 913870 57 7

All rights reserved. Reproduction in whole or in part in any form whatsoever or by any means is strictly prohibited without the prior permission of the Publisher.

Unless otherwise stated all images are the property of the author.

Typeset by SJmagic DESIGN SERVICES, India.

Contents

Introduction 4

PART 1 BRITISH MOTORCYCLES THROUGH THE DECADES

Chapter 1   Before the Beginning, 1853–1909 6

Chapter 2   The 1910s and World War One 9

Chapter 3   The 1920s 12

Chapter 4   The 1930s 15

Chapter 5   The 1940s and World War Two 18

Chapter 6   The 1950s 22

Chapter 7   The 1960s 25

Chapter 8   The 1970s 30

Chapter 9   The 1980s 35

PART 2 THE BRANDS

Chapter 10   Ariel Motorcycles 38

Chapter 11   BSA Motorcycles 44

Chapter 12   Matchless Motorcycles 51

Chapter 13   Norton Motorcycles 56

Chapter 14   Royal Enfield Motorcycles 64

Chapter 15   Triumph Motorcycles 69

Chapter 16   Velocette Motorcycles 80

Chapter 17   Vincent Motorcycles 85

PART 3 THE BITTER END AND BEYOND

Chapter 18   The Death of the British Motorcycle Industry 90

Chapter 19   Life After Death 94

Picture Credits 96

Introduction

The story of the classic British motorcycle itself, the industry that created them, and the culture that embraced them, is a fascinating tale full of highs and lows, victories and defeats, and innovation and obsolescence, with a little Greek tragedy thrown in for good measure.

Throughout the early 20th century, British motorcycles represented the leading edge of technology and performance, and by the mid-1950s the British were by far the largest producers of motorcycles in the world, and in some cases had achieved true industrial dominance well beyond just motorcycle production. Around this time, and until about 1968 (just before the introduction of the Honda CB750 changed everything), the hottest bikes on the road, mostly Triumphs, BSAs and Nortons, were all British. However, Royal Enfield, Matchless and AJS all made hot twins in the 1960s. These 500cc to 750cc twins were the period equivalent of today's modern sport bikes. They were fast, light and handled well. What else was there back then? Until Honda launched its 450cc dual overhead cam (DOHC) 'Black Bomber' in 1965, nothing from Japan had enough displacement to compete with the British, and most were 2-strokes. Harley-Davidson built a totally different type of motorcycle altogether; it was not meant to be thrown into corners on twisty mountain roads, and while powerful, it was much heavier. Europe made a few oddball bikes back then, very few of which made it out of Europe. Therefore, the British really didn't have any competition for the high-performance market, and their reputation grew. In 1960s America, if you wanted a fast, good-looking bike, you bought a Triumph 650 Bonneville or a Norton 750 Atlas.

The quintessential British motorcycle in the 1960s, the Triumph 650 Bonneville. This one is a 1965 Triumph T120R Bonneville, manufactured when Triumph was at the top of its game.

BSA entered the 1960s as not only the world's largest motorcycle company but also one of the largest companies of any kind, making everything from motorcycles, cars, trucks and buses to farm and heavy equipment, military vehicles, armaments, steel and more. It also built most of the world's best-selling motorcycles, yet, by the close of the decade, BSA was weak, broke and misguided, with a product line that was hopelessly outdated. By the end of 1967, the only British companies still making motorcycles were BSA, Triumph and Norton. BSA built their last motorcycle in 1972. By 1975, Norton stopped producing their one-and-only model, the Commando, leaving only Triumph as the last brand standing, and it was down to building just one model also: the 750 Bonneville. Production had dwindled down to nothing, and Triumph finally called it quits in 1983.

How these companies went from great heights to near-oblivion is a long and sordid story that begins with the Crimean War in 1856 and ends in Coventry, England, in 1983 when the last Triumph Bonneville rolled off the Meriden assembly line. The British motorcycle industry, once the great innovator and global leader, crumbled completely. Little remained, but that's another story.

This book will attempt to delve into the whole broad story, in the context of the times, while above all appreciating the beauty and engineering of these amazing motorcycles built by craftsmen in England.

The 1983 TRX was an eleventh-hour attempt at a factory custom, like Harley's Superglide. In their final year, Triumph produced several notable 'specials'.

PART 1: BRITISH MOTORCYCLES THROUGH THE DECADES

Chapter 1
Before the Beginning 1853–1909

BSA got its start making rifles for the British Army, beginning with the Crimean War in 1853.

The story of classic British motorcycles doesn't begin with motorcycles at all, or even with bicycles. It begins around 1760 with the birth of the Industrial Age in Great Britain, which was triggered by the invention of the steam engine. Soon, factories of every type began producing a wide range of products, in ever greater volumes, at ever lower prices (compared to handmade goods), all fuelled by Britain's copious coal reserves. By the mid-1800s, Britain was the dominant global player in virtually every area of endeavour: science, technology, manufacturing, finance, education, military and more.

Our story begins in 1853 in the Crimea in Eastern Europe. Great Britain was embroiled in a war with Russia, and it needed rifles. At the time, Britain was a powerhouse of innovation and manufacturing ability. However, this was still early in the Industrial Revolution, and many

Note that the BSA logo is a picture of three British Army rifles stacked together, paying homage to its birth as an arms maker.

Before cars and motorcycles, bicycles were all the rage in Britain, Europe and America. Many an entrepreneur entered the bicycle business, and some graduated into motorcycles around the turn of the 20th century.

manufactured items were still largely handmade by craftsmen. Firearms were no exception. A group of 16 small, independent gunmakers in Birmingham, England formed an alliance to produce the rifles needed for the British Army. Each little more than a cottage industry, using the most rudimentary production methods (mostly by hand), they together formed a production system that built rifles by the thousands during the Crimean War (1853–56).

This led to refinements and advancements in the manufacturing process, and by 1861 they formed the Birmingham Small Arms Company Ltd, or BSA for short. Its logo was in fact three rifles leaning together. With the support of the British government, a new factory was built in Small Heath and full-scale, modern (for the times) mass production of rifles was started, soon followed up by an expansion into munitions, all for the Crown.

The leadership of BSA, however, wanted not only to modernize its production methods but also to expand its product line. Soon, BSA was building a variety of products, and by 1884 it entered the burgeoning new bicycle market. It soon graduated up to motorised bicycles, and by 1905 had built its first true motorcycle. At this time, there were hundreds of cottage industries building, or trying to build, motorcycles, most using parts (like engines, gearboxes, wheels, etc) that were sourced elsewhere. By this time, BSA was a true industrial giant and was unique in the world as the only motorcycle manufacturer that built everything in-house.

Of course, BSA wasn't the only British bicycle company that evolved into motorcycle production, as many ambitious entrepreneurs followed suit. There was a bicycle boom going on, and many British companies that formed or expanded to produce bicycles in the late 1800s would very soon be building legendary motorcycles. Ariel made spoked bicycle wheels from 1870, later entire bicycles, then motorcycles starting in 1902; Matchless built bicycles in the late 1800s, then produced its first motorcycle in 1901; and Velocette started building bicycles in 1896 and motorcycles in 1904. Even the legendary Triumph started out building bicycles in 1884 and was building motorcycles by 1902, one year earlier than Harley-Davidson. It is noteworthy that around this same time, in America, the Wright brothers, who owned a bicycle shop, built the first successful powered aircraft, showing that the exploding bicycle market attracted all the best mechanical minds of their day.

The art and science of motorcycles advanced very quickly in the early 20th century. Advances in metallurgy, casting, forging, carburettors, ignition systems and more led to steady improvements in performance and reliability.

Hilda Pollitt was renowned as the first woman motorcyclist in England. Here she sits astride her new 1907 Douglas twin.

One of their earliest bikes, this 1903 Triumph 2½hp was state of the art for the times.

Chapter 2

The 1910s and World War One

This World War One-era British dispatch rider straddles a 'Trusty Triumph', so-named by British soldiers because of its ruggedness and reliability in battle.

Motorcycles were in their infancy, with many competing designs produced by hundreds of inventive entrepreneurs and companies large and small. Most of the weaker players, and the less-successful designs were soon gone. During this era, racing truly did improve the breed, with reliability as much as speed being tested on the track. Production bikes benefited greatly from the lessons learned in racing.

Just as things started getting interesting, Europe was thrust into yet another war between empires in 1914, and once again Britain needed supplies. BSA went right back to making more rifles, bullets, bombs and military vehicles, including 145,000 Lewis machine guns and, at its peak, 10,000 Lee-Enfield .303 rifles per week! However, it also built motorcycles for His Majesty's Army, as did Triumph, while Velocette and Vincent got some lucrative munitions contracts, but many of the others got nothing and were starved of raw materials during the war, struggling to remain open. BSA sailed through the war bigger and more profitable than ever, and Triumph gained a reputation in the field among the troops as 'The Trusty Triumph', known for its reliability and toughness.

1910s Stereotype

During the early 1910s, most motorcycles still had pedals. Around 1916, motorcycles began to change, to evolve, losing their pedals and flat tanks in favour of foot pegs and saddle tanks.

1911 was the first year for this AJS 292cc side-valve single. A racing version competed in the Isle of Man TT, where A J Stevens (after whom AJS was named) took 15th place in the Junior TT. This photo, of an unknown rider aboard a 1911 AJS, was taken in Queensland, Australia.

Rex was another small British motorcycle maker that didn't make it. This 1913 model features bicycle-style pedals and a JAP V-twin engine, in a bicycle-style diamond frame typical of the early 1910s.

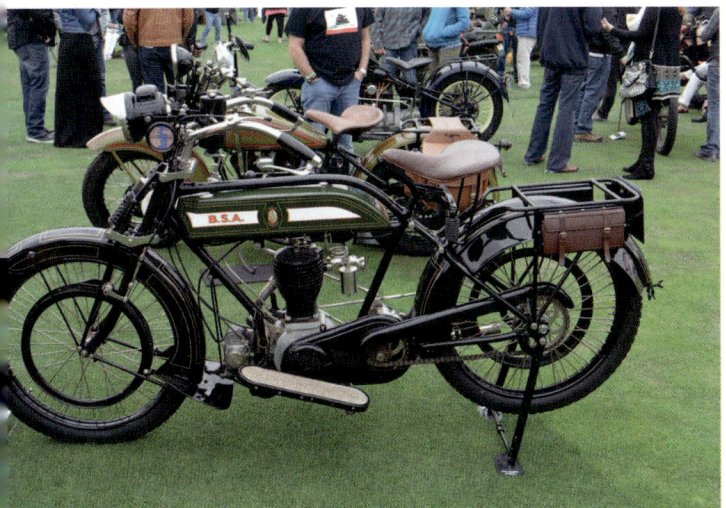

This 1916 BSA Model K bridged the gap between bicycles and modern motorcycles. It has lost its pedals and looks less bicycle-like.

During World War One, Royal Enfield built military motorcycles for the British War Department and for Imperial Russia. This is a 1915 Royal Enfield ambulance.

Chapter 3

The 1920s

In Europe, many families were too poor to own a car. Small, low-cost motorcycles filled the gap.

By the dawn of the 'Roaring Twenties', most manufacturers had settled into a few basic designs. Performance and reliability improved, as did brakes, suspension and electrics. More motorcycles lost their pedals and with them their 'bicycle-looks', as flat tanks disappeared in favour of more modern saddle tanks. Motorcycle racing gained in popularity. England teemed with racing motorcycles at places like the Isle of Man and Brooklands. Engine design advanced rapidly on the racetrack and on the street. Manufacturing methods were improving as well.

1920s Stereotype
By the end of the 1920s, a typical motorcycle was a 500cc or a larger single or V-twin flathead with a hand-shift/foot-clutch set-up, rigid frame and girder front forks.

Many larger, more affluent families graduated up to sidecars. This one is a 1927 Ariel Model B with a 550cc side-valve single-cylinder engine.

This 349cc side-valve 1924 AJS H4, with 3-speed hand-shifted gearbox, has an acetylene headlamp and tail light. By this time, AJS had vast racing experience, which showed in its street bikes.

This 1926 Royal Enfield 2¾hp Standard has a 350cc side-valve single-cylinder engine that made 2¾ horsepower. Note the hand shifter.

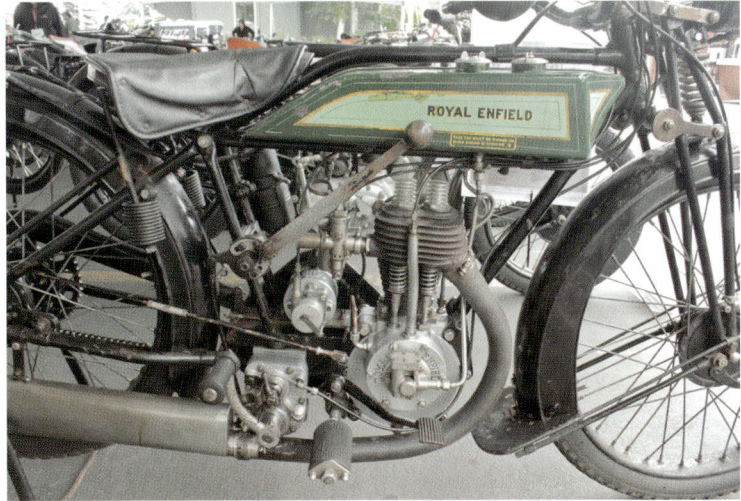

The 1928 Norton CS1 racer had Norton's first overhead cam (OHC) engine. The 500cc race bike was made famous in 1927 when Stanley Woods set an Isle of Man lap record of 70.99mph. This particular bike won the Veteran Old Timers' Race at the Isle of Man in 1948.

The 1920s was a time of great innovation and many different approaches were taken to the challenges the motorcycle industry faced. This 1927 Douglas shows how it overcame the vibration that haunted most brands: horizontally opposed cylinders.

Chapter 4

The 1930s

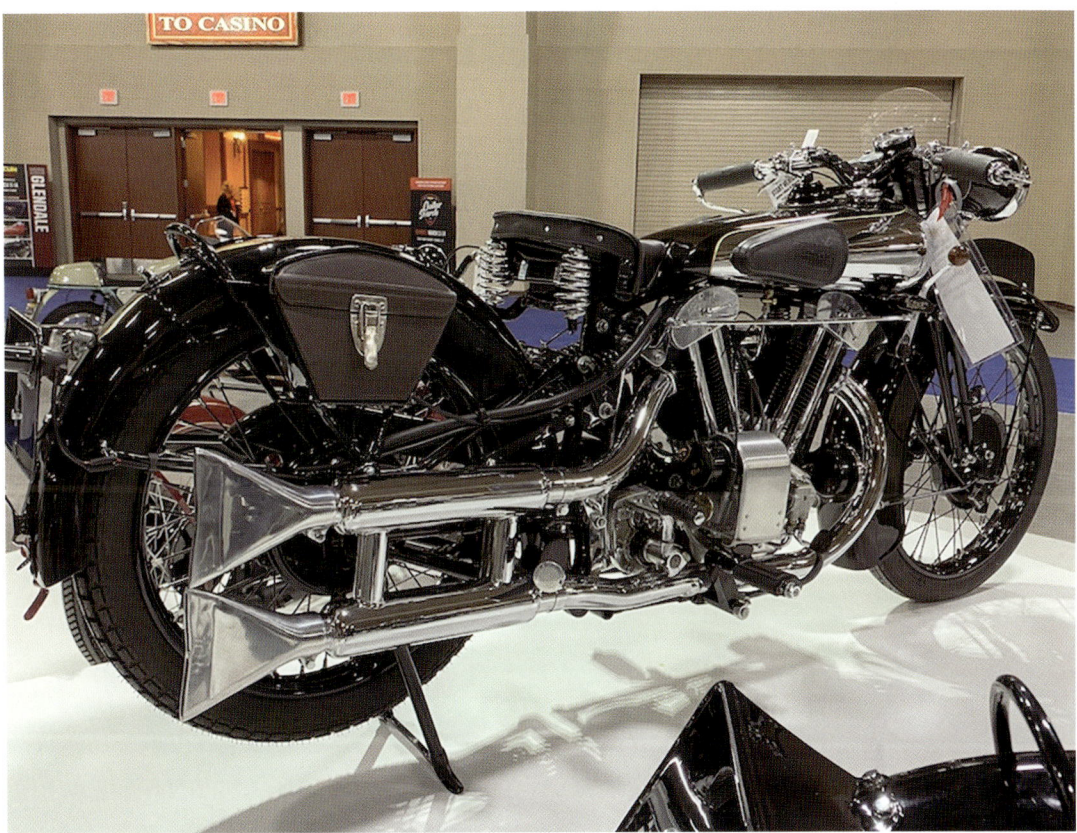

Brough Superior built some of the finest motorcycles in the world at the time. All of them came with engines sourced from other companies. This stunning 1930 SS100 used a 1,000cc JAP V-twin engine. The Brough became famous for being the motorcycle that Lawrence of Arabia rode.

The 1930s opened with the world in the depths of a gripping economic depression. Money was tight; most manufacturers struggled financially, and many failed. Against this backdrop, motorcycle racing was booming in America, in Europe and in Great Britain. New speed and endurance records were being set and broken.

Great design work flourished. Master engine designer Edward Turner began his career at Ariel, where he designed the first Square Four engine in 1931. When Ariel owner Jack Sangster bought a nearly bankrupt Triumph, he put Turner on to the task of spicing up their lacklustre product line. What resulted was an engine that changed the world: the first parallel twin (aka vertical twin), in the 1938 500cc Speed Twin. This at a time when most of the rest of the industry was fixated on big singles and V-twins. The vertical twin was light, compact, liked to rev and made great power. Just as things got going, World War Two started and diverted all industrial production over to support the war effort.

1930s Stereotype

The average late 1930s British motorcycle was a 350cc single-cylinder 4-stroke with overhead valves (OHV), a 3-speed gearbox, a rigid frame and a girder front end.

The 1938 Triumph 500 Speed Twin is one of the world's most pivotal motorcycles, historically. With it, genius engine designer Edward Turner introduced a single-cylinder world to the vertical twin, and soon nearly every other British brand rushed to follow. Note the girder front forks. All pre-war bikes had them, but by the war's end, most switched to telescopic front forks.

This 1933 Velocette KTT was fairly typical of road racers in the 1930s: 500cc single, rigid frame, girder front forks. However, one thing set it apart from the others: it had an OHC that was shaft-driven with bevel gears.

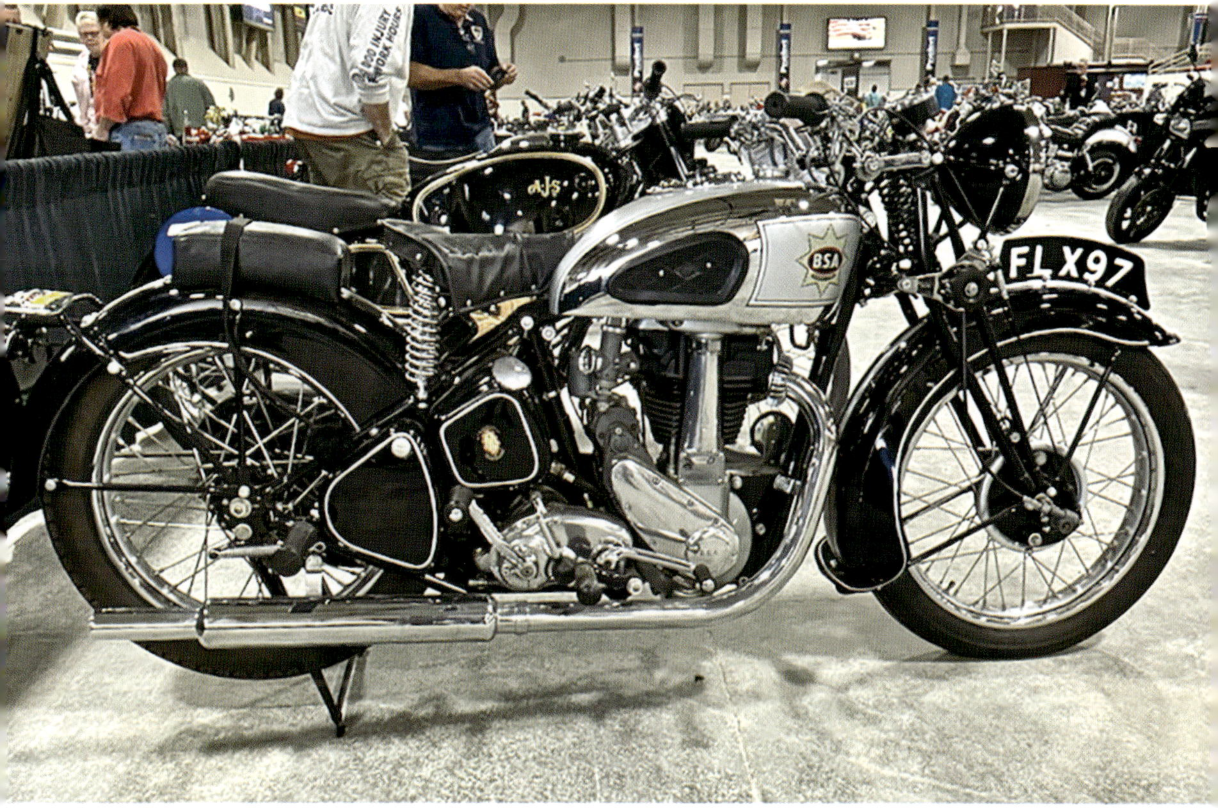

The 500cc BSA Silver Star served as the springboard into BSA's legendary racer, the Gold Star. This is a 1939 Silver Star.

One of the most elegant and best engineered motorcycles of its time was the 998cc Vincent V-twin. This one is a 1938 Vincent Rapide.

The 1939 Matchless Model X was intended for sidecar duty, with its torquey 982cc V-twin engine. Big, understressed side-valve (flathead) V-twins were standard fare for growing families graduating from a motorcycle to a sidecar rig.

Chapter 5

The 1940s and World War Two

BSA built 130,000 M20 500cc side-valve singles during World War Two. This one is a 1945 model.

Britain adopted a wartime footing in 1939, and by 1940, most motorcycle manufacturers were given government contracts, some to build motorcycles and others to build weapons, munitions and anything else needed to help win the war. Once again, BSA became the biggest beneficiary of this, selling 130,000 M20 military motorcycles, endless Lee-Enfield rifles and, at its peak, 16,390 Browning machine guns per month! Again, it sailed out of the war fat and happy, with huge factories ready to produce consumer goods again.

In 1940, Triumph's Coventry factory was bombed by the Germans during the Blitz, destroying it. A new factory was built in Meriden by 1942.

At the end of the war, everyone scrambled to get back into the motorcycle business, some on a better footing than others. BSA did well, but most others struggled to get going again. Fortunately, the

The Royal Enfield 'Flying Flea' was a lightweight military bike designed to parachute in with airborne troops giving them greater mobility behind enemy lines. After the war, it became a popular low-priced commuter in the UK.

market for motorcycles was red hot as soldiers returned home to the UK looking for wives, homes, jobs and transportation. However, unlike America, Britain came out of the war economically devastated, and times were tough for the average Briton. This, coupled with narrow roads, low-quality petrol and high prices for fuel, meant that many British people couldn't afford a car. Many rode motorcycles, and if they had a growing family, a sidecar as well.

Most manufacturers revived pre-war designs, but those that could afford to, advanced their suspension designs from girder front ends to telescopic forks, first introduced by Matchless and AJS in 1941. Triumph relaunched its 500cc 1946 Speed Twin, and nearly the entire industry followed suit, those that could afford it, anyway. Similar to how the Japanese air-cooled 4-cylinder was the standard of the industry in the 1980s, by the close of the 1940s, the vertical twin was the engine design of choice for manufacturers, on the racetrack and out in the marketplace, in Britain at least.

1940s Stereotype

By the end of the 1940s, the mainstream British motorcycle was an OHV 500cc vertical twin with a 4-speed gearbox, a rigid frame and telescopic front forks.

By the time the Triumph Speed Twin went back into production after the war (1946), the old girder fork was gone, replaced by modern telescopic front forks. Most other brands did the same.

The quintessential Matchless single. Matchless and AJS singles are nearly identical mechanically. The only difference is that Matchless locates the magneto behind the cylinder and AJS puts it in front. This is a 1948 Matchless G80 500cc single.

The 500cc 1946 Velocette KSS had an OHC driven by a shaft with bevel gears. Elegant but expensive to produce.

One of the most unique and innovative British bikes of the era was the 487cc Sunbeam S7. It had two parallel cylinders one in front of the other, with the crankshaft oriented longitudinally, instead of across the frame like most bikes. They were very smooth. BSA bought the Sunbeam brand in 1943. This is a 1948 Sunbeam S7.

This 1947 Ariel Red Hunter was very much a blueprint for what a British single was like in the late 1940s: 500cc pushrod single, rigid rear frame and telescopic front forks. It was Ariel's biggest seller.

Chapter 6

The 1950s

During the 1950s, motorcycling was changing from low-cost, basic transportation to a recreational sport. A combination of factors contributed to this, including an improving economy and the growing 'youth market'. Motorcycling developed more as a culture than ever before.

The 1950s certainly were the heyday for the British motorcycle industry. They literally owned the motorcycle market, much the same way the Japanese took over the American market in the 1970s. In both cases, what buyers wanted were fast, good-looking bikes.

Triumph fired the first salvo in the horsepower wars by boring and stroking out its 500 twin to stretch it into the 650cc Triumph 6T Thunderbird in 1950, and again, the industry followed suit. Displacement and horsepower grew sharply. By around 1953, most British manufacturers had adopted a swingarm rear suspension set-up. Throughout the 1950s, most companies played catch up with Triumph, in both displacement and horsepower. In 1959, Triumph did it again by offering twin carburettors on its popular 650 twin, with the introduction of the legendary Bonneville.

While the biggest market for British motorcycles had, for decades, been the British home market, by the late 1950s, it was increasingly becoming America. Americans were hungry for speed and style, and the British supplied both, in spades.

1950s Stereotype

By the close of the 1950s, the average British bike was a 650cc vertical twin with a 4-speed gearbox, swingarm rear suspension and telescopic front forks.

The 1950 Triumph 6T Thunderbird is one of the most important bikes of the 1950s. It was the first of the British vertical twins to bump displacement from 500cc to 650cc, and it set off an arms race that never stopped.

This 1954 BSA A10 Golden Flash 650 twin was typical of the steady improvement in motorcycles throughout this time, in displacement, performance and style.

The mighty BSA Gold Star was a hit on the street, on the track and in showrooms. This 1956 'Goldie' is a street version, but stripped-down racers dominated desert racing throughout the 1950s and early 1960s.

Bikes like this 1958 Ariel H5 Mk 3 proved that the big British single was still alive and well in the late-1950s. They were more popular in Britain than in speed-crazed America, however.

The 1958 AJS Model 31CS was one of a pair of hot 650 twins from AMC, the Matchless G12 and the AJS Model 31. They were well-built bikes but couldn't compete against the combined might of Triumph and BSA. They'd already punched them out to the 650cc here from their 500cc origins and would stretch them out yet again in 1961, taking them to 750cc.

Chapter 7

The 1960s

By the 1960s, a whole new consumer market was opening up in Britain, Europe and especially in America. They called it the 'youth market'. 'Baby boomers', born right after World War Two, were now coming of age, and because of the prosperity boom in America and elsewhere, these kids had buying power. Motorcycles were red hot! However, Indian Motorcycles had failed in the 1950s, leaving Harley-Davidson as the only US motorcycle manufacturer. Harley had, however, garnered a bad rep in the 1950s, as it was associated with outlaw gangs and hooligans. Honda went in the other direction with their bold ad campaign, 'You meet the nicest people on a Honda'. Somewhere in the vast gulf between the two, in the middle of the market, the British found their place. They were in an ideal position to capitalise on this burgeoning youth market. Their bikes were the right size; they were fast, sexy and already well accepted in the American marketplace. The big British brands were on top of the world.

BSA entered the 1960s as the world's largest producer of motorcycles, and it owned Triumph, also one of the biggest producers. AMC (Associated Motor Cycles, not American Motors) had grown into another British motorcycle powerhouse, having accumulated the brands Norton, Matchless, AJS, James and Francis-Barnett. Nortons were selling well, and Matchless and AJS singles were still a prime choice for off-road and racing.

However, times were changing. The Japanese had gained a foothold in the US market and were steadily getting

By the opening of the 1960s, motorcycling had almost fully moved from a cheap form of transportation to a recreational lifestyle, being driven largely by the burgeoning youth market, now of buying age.

The 1965 Honda 450 'Black Bomber' was the first Japanese bike big and powerful enough to challenge the British at their own game. It was just the beginning.

The 1969 Honda CB750 Four shocked the world! It was so much bike for the money, and cost less than the British Triples, without the oil spots in the driveway. It was a true game-changer.

better and better, and they were building bigger and bigger bikes. In the early 1960s, Japanese bikes (other than Honda) were generally 2-strokes and were quite small, almost always under 250cc. Honda broke the mould in 1965 with the introduction of their DOHC 450cc 'Black Bomber'. It was a high-tech tour de force with an all-aluminium, diecast twin-cylinder engine with dual OHCs, torsion bars for valve springs, two constant-velocity carburettors, and lots of power. They were also totally reliable, and never leaked oil, which were common complaints about British bikes. They were at least as fast as most British 650s, and in many cases faster, and it wouldn't stop there. The Japanese were just getting started.

Meanwhile, back in England, trouble was brewing. Most of the off-brands had failed or were on the verge of failure. Only Triumph, BSA and Norton seemed to fare well, but they were being produced in tiny quantities compared to the mass production pouring out of Japan. In 1951, Jack Sangster, owner of Ariel, who at the time also owned Triumph, made a deal with BSA, selling both brands in exchange for a seat on BSA's board of directors. He soon became chairman of the board. He spent the late 1950s and early 1960s dismantling BSA and selling off its parts. He stripped it down to the bare bones, presumably enriching himself.

Just as all other British brands were getting weak, suddenly BSA was the only truly big player in the market, and it was struggling. AMC dropped everything but the Norton Commando, which sold well but in small numbers. As people began to realise that they could have style and performance without the reliability issues, the oil leaks and the vibration, they started buying Japanese bikes instead of British iron or Harleys.

In 1968, Honda announced its radical new 4-cylinder CB750, which launched as a 1969 model. It absolutely changed the world. Triumph and BSA had been slow to come to market with their own multis: the 3-cylinder Triumph Trident and BSA Rocket 3. Stunning achievements for the British, fine bikes to be sure but not enough to offset the mighty Honda. The introduction of the CB750 is widely regarded as the death knell for the British motorcycle industry. It just went downhill from there.

1960s Stereotype

By the close of the 1960s, British bikes as a whole had been eclipsed by the tsunami of cheap, high-quality bikes pouring out of Japan. Most of the lesser brands were gone by this time: AJS, Ariel, Matchless, Royal Enfield, Velocette and Vincent had all disappeared. Only Triumph, BSA and Norton remained, building fewer and fewer bikes. 1970 is considered by many to be the Triumph 650's zenith; Norton's 750 Commando was still ripping, although in low numbers, and Triumph and BSA had their incredible 750 triples, the Triumph Trident and the BSA Rocket 3, along with a mix of middleweights and lightweights. But again, nothing was selling in nearly the volumes that was needed for the British motorcycle industry to survive, much less prosper and advance against the onslaught from the East. The crop of 1970 British bikes may have been the best they'd ever had, perhaps the best they ever would have, at least to some. Unfortunately, is was still too little, too late.

The Triumph 650 Bonneville was the hottest bike of its era, the equivalent of today's sport bikes. Fast, light and handsome, with great handling and loads of 'cool'. What made the Bonneville so hot? Twin carburettors. This is a 1962 model.

The Royal Enfield 750 Interceptor was an excellent bike for the times but only at fairly low production numbers. Their reputation for leaking oil gained them the nickname 'Royal Oilfield', but otherwise, they were fast, solid, well-made machines.

This 650cc 1965 BSA A65 Spitfire Mk II was one of the stars of BSA's line-up. Dual carburettors, down pipes, flashy styling, strong performance – it had it all.

Classic British Motorcycles

Yet another hot new model spun off Norton's venerable twin that started out life in 1949 at 500cc, and by 1973 had been stretched to 850cc. This 1969 Norton 650SS was seriously fast and remained in production beyond the launch of the Commando in 1969.

The 1969 Triumph Trident (and its sister bike, the BSA Rocket 3) was a stunning achievement by any standard, much less for an industry so close to collapse. It was fast and handled well, but at first, it was kind of homely, with its 'shoebox' gas tanks and 'ray gun' mufflers.

BSA owned Triumph and so insisted that BSA have a triple as well, but it had to look different. So, while the Trident had vertical cylinders, they slanted forward by 12 degrees on the 1969 BSA Rocket 3. This required all-new bottom cases, a very expensive endeavour, and it slowed development such that both triples launched just weeks before the Honda CB750.

Norton launched its game-changing 750 Commando in 1969 with more power but an effective solution to the vibration problem: isolastic suspension. It rubber mounted the engine and swingarm. It was smooth, powerful, handled better than just about any other bike on the street, and it was sexy. This is a 1969 Commando Fastback. It came in several styles.

Of the plethora of British bikes that entered the decade, by the close of the 1960s, only the Commando, a few Triumphs and BSAs remained. At the top of the heap, by sales anyway, was the Triumph 650 (TR6 and Bonneville combined). This one is a 1970 Triumph T120R Bonneville.

Chapter 8
The 1970s

As 1970 dawned, the only three British motorcycle manufacturers still standing were BSA, Triumph and Norton. It was only natural that the three former competitors would try to team up. But would it be enough?

In 1971, BSA (which owned Triumph) made the controversial move of remodelling its entire heavyweight product line, and that of Triumph, with a new oil-bearing frame and running gear. At a time when BSA and Triumph were suffering from vibration, reliability issues, electrical problems,

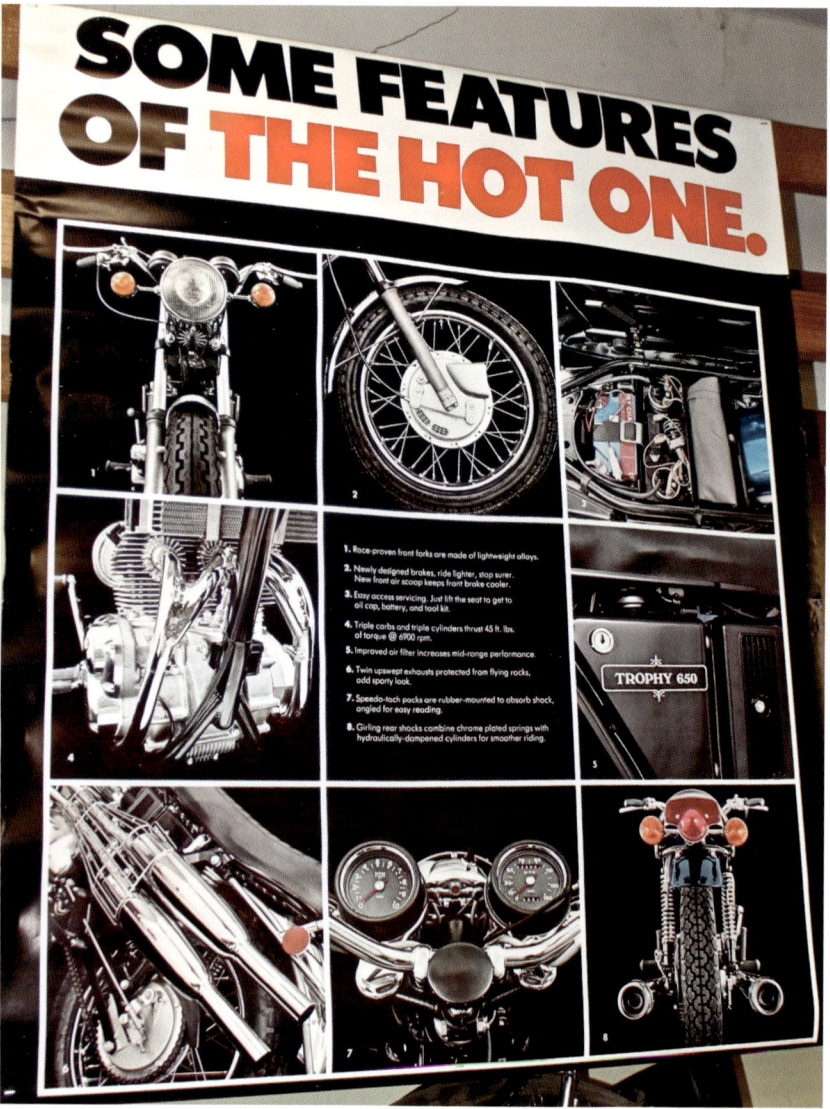

This Triumph dealership poster promoted Triumph's new 1971 motorcycles. A combination of obsolete engine designs and manufacturing, high prices due to a poor exchange rate and blistering competition from Japan caused the new bikes to struggle on the market. It didn't help that Japanese bikes had OHCs, electric starters, 5-speed gearboxes and front disc brakes, all things that didn't exist on Triumphs in 1971.

oil leaks and above all, obsolete engine designs, they didn't do a thing to solve any of those problems. Instead, they designed a whole new frame, with the oil contained in the 3-inch diameter backbone instead of in an oil tank. It was shared by both Triumph's and BSA's 650 twins, using the same old engines. BSA had done such a bad job of it that when the new frames hit the Meriden assembly line, workers found that the Triumph engines wouldn't fit into the frames in one piece. They had to be partially disassembled, installed, then reassembled on the production line!

They were good-looking bikes, but they didn't move the needle enough to counter the tidal wave from Honda and other Japanese manufacturers. The new look, however, actually turned off many traditional Triumph and BSA buyers. By this time, the Triumph and BSA triples had matured and were turning into fine machines, but because of the valuation of the British pound at that time, the bikes were more expensive than the Honda CB750, even though the Honda had an electric starter, 5-speed gearbox, a front disc brake and another cylinder! It is noteworthy, however, that the British Triples were lighter and actually quicker than the big Honda and handled much better than the bloated 4-cylinder.

By the end of 1972, BSA stopped building motorcycles. It had cut a deal with AMC (which owned Norton) to form a new company called NVT (Norton-Villiers-Triumph) that joined BSA, Triumph and Norton together under one conglomerate. It made perfect sense, but alas it was too little too late. BSA collapsed and Norton ended up owning Triumph.

By 1971, the BSA Rocket 3 had lost its dorky bodywork and turned into a handsome brute. Note the conical brakes and the dove grey frame.

The Norton Commando came in many body styles over its short life: Roadster, Fastback, Interstate, Hi-Rider, JPN, Production Racers and Combat. Other than the Combat, all were essentially stock Commandos with different bodywork. This is a 1972 Norton Commando Roadster.

Yamaha introduced its XS650 in 1973, which was the Japanese take on the classic vertical twin. Yamaha just perfected it. This is a 1977.

When the new owners arrived at Triumph's Meriden factory to tell them they were moving all production to Norton's Donington factory in an effort to cut costs, the Triumph workers rebelled, barricaded themselves in the plant and wouldn't let anything come in or go out for most of the 1974 model year. As a result, very few 1974 Bonnevilles were ever built. 1974 Trident production continued unabated as it was built in BSA's Small Heath plant, where it used to be built together with the Rocket 3. After much drama, back-and-forth and gnashing of teeth, the strike was finally resolved in 1975 by forming a new worker-owned organisation called the Meriden Co-op. They were undercapitalised from the start and struggled along, making fewer and fewer bikes each year, then down to just Tridents and Bonnevilles. Norton was doing well enough, albeit in small volumes. However, even it couldn't keep going. It built the last Commando in 1975.

The Japanese, meanwhile, were producing bikes in record numbers, and in an ever-widening variety. Kawasaki followed Honda's lead and broke out of the 2-stroke business, building the 900cc DOHC 4-cylinder Z1. It was pretty much game over for the beleaguered British, and it only went downhill from there. Suzuki and Yamaha, both having built only 2-stroke bikes, moved into the 4-stroke market. Yamaha even had the audacity to out-British the British, with a 650cc vertical twin in the classic British mould, except that it was built like a Japanese bike. An all-alloy, diecast OHC engine, 5-speed gearbox, an electric starter and a level of build quality that the British couldn't seem to approach. The 1969 Yamaha XS650 got it right.

1970s Stereotype

By the close of the 1970s, the only British bike still in production was the Triumph 750 Bonneville. During the 1970s, however, Norton played an important role; BSA built some bikes at the start of the decade and Triumph produced Tridents until 1975 and introduced many special models of the Bonneville in a vain effort to boost sales.

With vibration, electrical and reliability problems to deal with, Triumph and BSA put their meagre resources into a new frame and running gear for their 1971 650 twins. Long-time Triumph loyalists didn't like the look of the new bike, but it was a handsome machine, brought up to date styling-wise. Not very collectable, but they're probably the best-riding Triumphs.

This 1975 Norton 850 Commando Roadster carries the 'Union Jack' paint scheme. 1975 was the last year of Commando production.

The 1973 Triumph X-75 Hurricane has quite a story. It was designed by American fairing pioneer Craig Vetter for BSA, which wanted to one-up Triumph. Alas, before it could be released, BSA was out of business and Triumph inherited the project. Despite having a BSA engine and frame, it was launched as a one-year-only Triumph. Only 1,172 were built. Today, they are very collectable.

The legendary Rickman brothers built their incredible motocross bikes with a variety of engines throughout the 1970s. They were famous for their gorgeous nickel-plated frames with perfect welding beads. This one is a 1970 Rickman BSA, using a BSA 441 Victor engine.

The 1969 movie *Easy Rider* kicked off the chopper craze, and this was Norton's response. The 1971 Norton Hi-Rider had high 'ape-hanger' handlebars and a ridiculous banana seat with sissy bar. Many buyers swapped the goofy parts for normal Commando fare, and so today, original Hi-Riders are much sought-after by collectors.

The 1971 BSA B50 MX was a brawny 500cc single and was considered to be the successor to the legendary Gold Star. It was a very respectable dirt bike in the open class, mostly because of its handling because the heavy 4-stroke struggled to keep up with lighter, more powerful 2-strokes. It was one of the last bikes that BSA built.

Chapter 9

The 1980s

The 1980s opened with only one motorcycle still in production in all of the UK, the evergreen Triumph Bonneville. This one is a 1980 T140E (the 'E' stands for Environmental, meaning detuned for smog purposes).

By 1980, the only British motorcycle still in production was the Triumph 750 Bonneville, which was using essentially the same engine design that Edward Turner had created back in 1937. This, against a never-ending onslaught of bigger, better and faster bikes out of Japan.

The Meriden Co-op sought government help and assistance from investors, but no one answered. The British government, at this time controlled by the Socialist Party, had no patience for businesses and let them flap in the wind. It got so bad for Triumph that many suppliers stopped sending parts for fear of non-payment. Triumph was forced to look elsewhere for its tanks, mirrors, lights and switchgear. It found them in Italy. However, even this didn't last, as sales continued to slide, and the money wasn't coming in. By 1983, the Meriden Co-op couldn't take another step. It slid into receivership and ended Triumph's illustrious legacy... almost.

A billionaire British real estate developer named John Bloor bought the company out of bankruptcy for a song, with plans to revive the brand with modernised versions of their classic bikes. This would take years to pull off, and he didn't want to lose the unbroken chain of production, which started in 1902 (making it the world's oldest continuously operating motorcycle manufacturer), so he sold the rights to the Bonneville, and the tooling to make them, to Les Harris. Harris continued hand-building Bonnevilles in England until 1990, when Bloor was ready to reintroduce the Triumph brand to the world.

From a new, state-of-the-art factory in Hinkley, England, thoroughly modern Triumph motorcycles started rolling off the assembly line in 1990, and they sell like hotcakes to a whole new generation of enthusiasts. Modern Triumphs come in 2-, 3- and 4-cylinder designs, and their quality, style and performance are on par with the best motorcycles in the world today.

After the Commando, Norton moved into rotary-powered (Wankel) motorcycles and built a series of them throughout the 1980s and into the 1990s, albeit in triple-digit quantities at best. This is a 1989 Norton F1 Rotary.

Finally, after all these years, a Triumph twin with an electric starter, dubbed 'Electro'. A large growth appeared on the timing cover, which was reminiscent of the old magneto drives, which housed the new starter drive. Unfortunately, Lucas built the starters, so they only worked at random. Modern upgrades have solved that issue. This is a 1982 Triumph Bonneville Electro.

In a desperate last gasp, the scrappy lads at Triumph proved they could accomplish great things with few resources. The 1983 Triumph TSS adopted a Westlake-designed 8-valve head (4 valves-per-cylinder), electric start, a new forged steel crank and rods, mag wheels and bold styling. They made 58 horsepower without most of the vibration that plagued vertical twins for decades. Only 438 were built.

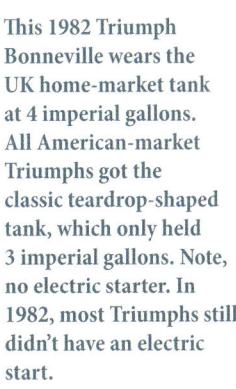

This 1982 Triumph Bonneville wears the UK home-market tank at 4 imperial gallons. All American-market Triumphs got the classic teardrop-shaped tank, which only held 3 imperial gallons. Note, no electric starter. In 1982, most Triumphs still didn't have an electric start.

PART 2: THE BRANDS
Chapter 10
Ariel Motorcycles

Who was Jack Sangster?

The Ariel Motorcycle Company, while never a stunning success itself, built a few memorable bikes, including the legendary Ariel Square Four, albeit it in fairly low numbers. Its was a story like so many other classic British motorcycle makers, with one enormous difference: Jack Sangster. Sangster gained entry into the motorcycle industry through his father's purchase of the ailing Ariel Cycle Co., climbed to the absolute peak of that industry, then ended up, perhaps more than any other single person, gutting and destroying it. Hence, the following is as much a study of Ariel Motorcycles as it is an indictment of Sangster's role in the ultimate demise of not just Ariel, but BSA, Triumph, and whatever was left of the British motorcycle industry by 1970.

As chairman of the board at BSA, Jack Sangster oversaw the stripping and selling off of BSA's wealth, talent and assets. By the time he retired in 1961, BSA was too shaky to face the coming challenge from Japan.

The Early Days at Ariel

Like so many other classic British motorcycle companies of the era, Ariel started out as a bicycle manufacturer, or, more precisely, it built the wire-spoked wheels for bicycles under the first such patent issued in England, under the name Ariel Cycle Co. Established in England in 1870 by James Starley and William Hillman, it was soon building entire bicycles and also sewing machines, but the bicycles of the era were the type with the huge front wheel and tiny back wheel, with the pedals on the front axle. In 1885, Starley's nephew, John Kemp Starley, invented the first 'modern' bicycle with two similar-sized wheels and a chain driving the rear wheel, essentially what we use today. Ariel was the first! By 1898, it was shoe-horning engines into things, its first attempt being a tricycle with a 2¼hp De Dion engine. It took until 1902 for Ariel to build its first true motorcycle, using an engine purchased from an engine manufacturer, a very common practice among early motorcycle builders. In this case, the Kerry engine was very innovative for the era, with a new-for-the-times magneto and a carburettor with a float.

This 1908 Ariel 3hp shows just how early Ariel got into the motorcycle game. Note the bicycle pedals.

Sangster Takes Over Ariel

That same year, Ariel, still a very small company, was taken over by Components Ltd, which was owned by Charles Sangster. He immediately started building a 2-stroke motorcycle with a 3-speed gearbox, which he named the 'Arielette'. Production ceased with the outbreak of World War One. In 1918, Sangster's son, Jack, took over management of the Ariel division of Components Ltd and oversaw the introduction of a new bike using a White and Poppe 4-stroke engine that proved successful. He quickly expanded Ariel's model line-up with bikes ranging in size from 586cc to 992cc, using outsourced engines. Starting in 1926, Ariel began designing and building its own engines. The younger Sangster had lured legendary engine designer Val Page away from JAP, and the results were immediate. Page created two new engines and one entire motorcycle by 1927. This basic engine design, introduced in the 1926–30 Black Ariel was the basis for nearly every Ariel 4-stroke single-cylinder engine from then on. Its slogan around this time was 'The Modern Motor Cycle'.

Early Ariel Square Fours featured Edward Turner-designed 500cc and 600cc OHC engines. Complexity and cooling problems led to a switch over to the 1,000cc OHV engine in 1937. This is a 1932 Ariel Square Four with an OHC 600cc engine.

Square Four

The Square Four was completely redesigned in 1937 as an all-aluminium OHV 1,000cc four-cylinder. This is a 1953 Ariel Square Four.

During this time, parent company Components Ltd was having financial troubles, including numerous spells of receivership from 1911 to 1932 when it finally went bankrupt and closed its doors. Jack Sangster seized upon the opportunity to buy Ariel Motorcycles at a bargain price from the receivers, renamed it Ariel Motors, built a new factory in Birmingham and resumed production. By this time, he'd taken on another promising designer, Edward Turner, who had just come up with a radical new design for an OHC 4-cylinder bike that placed the four vertical cylinders in a square pattern, running on two parallel counter-rotating crankshafts, one in front of the other, that were geared together. The 500cc Ariel Square Four was introduced in 1931. The company went broke again, and wheeler-dealer Sangster reopened once more under yet another name. Production resumed on the now-600cc Square Four. Constant overheating problems with the rear cylinders led to a complete redesign in 1937 to the OHV 995cc model 4G.

Sangster Buys Triumph for a Song

In 1936, Triumph Motorcycles, also on hard times financially, in the midst of the Great Depression, went into receivership and Jack Sangster bought this legendary brand for a mere £50,000. Now he owned two motorcycle companies. He brought young Turner over from Ariel to help juice up Triumph's ailing motorcycle line-up. Turner wasted no time, completely designing, producing and introducing the 500cc 5T Speed Twin by 1937, as a 1938 model. It was a game-changer: the world's first vertical twin of its type, and it set the pattern for nearly every British twin for the next 40 years.

This 1956 Ariel Square Four shows the beauty of this massive engine. Their counter-rotating crankshafts made them incredibly smooth and torquey. However, their head design doomed them to touring duty, because they weren't very fast.

The Ariel Red Hunter is Born

Val Page had designed a new single-cylinder engine, which was introduced in 1932 as the Ariel Red Hunter, a name and a bike that would stay in production until 1959. During this time, it was available as a 250, 350 and 500. They performed brilliantly and sold very well, becoming Ariel's strongest product. The income derived from Red Hunter sales allowed Sangster to buy Triumph. Like everyone else, Ariel ceased civilian production with the outbreak of World War Two, to build boatloads of W/NG 350cc military bikes, which featured added ground clearance, among other upgrades. After the war, Ariel went back to making Square Fours and Red Hunters.

Ariel's Red Hunter 500 single was by far their biggest seller. This is a 1947 Ariel Red Hunter.

Sangster Sells Ariel and Triumph to BSA

In 1944, Sangster sold Ariel to BSA. After the war, Triumph was doing so well in the growing motorcycle market, and the new all-important US export market, that Sangster sold Triumph to BSA for £2.5 million, a tidy return on his £50,000 investment. BSA was not only the world's largest and richest motorcycle company at the time; but it was also one of the largest companies of any kind. BSA was a true multi-national corporate giant. It built not only motorcycles, but also cars, buses, trucks, military vehicles, industrial, construction, agricultural and mining equipment, armaments, munitions, steel and more. Its steel-making was considered state-of-the-art at the time, and its metallurgists were among the best. It seemed the company could accomplish anything. BSA was flush with cash, credit, resources, manpower, brainpower and vast market reach. So, Sangster smartly made his installation onto BSA's board of directors part of the Triumph deal. If BSA wanted Triumph, Jack Sangster had to come along as part of the package.

Ariel got into the vertical twin business with bikes like this 650cc 1958 Ariel Cyclone. Buddy Holly owned one.

This shot of a 1956 Square Four with its valve cover removed shows the basic cylinder-head layout. Here you can see the eight vertical valves, easier for production, but not conducive to high performance. All the pushrods come up between the front and back row of cylinders, and the whole thing is fed by a single carburettor breathing through a long intake port running down the middle of the head. They were smooth, but they weren't fast.

Ariel Product Development

Under BSA's tutelage, Ariel continued along producing low numbers of the Square Four and high volumes of Red Hunter singles. The Square Four was never a great performance bike. It was heavy; the rear cylinders still tended to run hot, even after several design upgrades. The valves were all situated vertically, car-style, rather than angled like more modern designs, and all four cylinders were fed by one single carburettor, with a long and tortuous intake tract. All of this restricted airflow, limiting its maximum performance potential. Not to mention those two heavy crankshafts. However, they were very smooth and provided excellent low-end torque, which made them ideal for sidecar duty. The Red Hunter, on the other hand, was fast and sold well through the 1950s, until big singles all began to fade from glory with the advent of the vertical twin. With BSA's help, Ariel came out with its own vertical twin, the 500cc Model KH, and the 650cc Huntmaster, both with engines based on the BSA A10. Badge-engineering had arrived at Ariel. Typical of Ariel Motorcycles overall, the new twins were well designed and well built and pretty fast. The Huntmaster was capable of 100mph in the early 1950s, a fact that still didn't bring in the much-needed sales the company was hoping for. Even the famous Square Four was a slow-seller, totalling just 15,639 units over its entire 28-year lifespan (1931–59).

Misreading the Market

By the late 1950s, ailing Ariel needed to do something fast, and fortunately parent company BSA still had the resources to do it. However, designing, testing, developing, then tooling up for and producing an all-new motorcycle was a huge commitment in time, energy and money, even for a giant like BSA. Therefore, the question was, what to do? Throughout the 1950s, the British home market for inexpensive commuter bikes had been growing steadily among the rising middle class who couldn't yet afford a car. Lightweight 2-strokes like the BSA Bantam were selling more and more with each passing year. Ariel, and parent company BSA, thought this trend would keep on growing forever. What they didn't count on was the 1959 BMC Mini, a 4-passenger car that didn't cost much more than a motorcycle, and suddenly Britain abandoned commuter bikes for microcars. However, the die had already been cast, and Ariel was already well into the development process of its two new models. Both were 250cc 2-stroke twins, one with fully enclosed bodywork called the Leader, and the other, without it, called the Arrow. Both were huge flops in the marketplace and proved to be the final nail in Ariel's coffin. BSA closed the Ariel factory at Selly Oak in 1962, moving remaining Leader and Arrow production to BSA's own factory at Small Heath, until the last true Ariel was built in 1965. The market

Ariel thought this bike was the future. Admittedly, this 1961 Ariel Leader made an attractive package.

they had built the bikes for had shrunk down to nearly nothing, and the recent onslaught of high-quality, low-priced bikes from Japan had rendered them obsolete and totally uncompetitive.

Sangster Cashes in BSA's Chips

But, what of Jack Sangster? Following a series of boardroom battles, and plenty of behind-the-scenes manoeuvring, Sangster succeeded in ousting BSA's chairman of the board, Sir Bernard Docker, in 1956. He installed himself as the new chairman, and over the next several years, presided over the stripping and selling-off of the BSA industrial empire. Factories, research centres, steel mills and valuable contracts were all sold off, making BSA weaker by the year. Of course, the 1950s were the best of times for the two biggest players in the British motorcycle business: BSA (which included BSA, Triumph, Ariel and Sunbeam) and AMC (which built Matchless, AJS, Norton, James and Francis-Barnett), so no one seemed to notice or mind. However, by the time Jack Sangster retired from the board of BSA in 1961, this once mighty industrial powerhouse was weak, broke, behind the market technologically and clueless as to what to do about it. Where did all the money from the sale of all of its assets go? Certainly not back into the company. Jack Sangster probably did well, but he left BSA crippled beyond repair. BSA had been the strongest player in the marketplace, perhaps the only one strong enough to stand up to the upcoming Japanese invasion in their pre-Sangster condition. However, that was mainly because BSA owned Triumph, and Triumph was enjoying great success, especially in America, right up to about 1970. But that's another story. If BSA had remained strong and had kept the brainpower that it had (many of its best people left the company in disgust during those years), it could have embraced and leveraged Triumph's US success and poured the much-needed funds into a new line of modern engines, more akin to what the Japanese were building. Of course, this never happened. BSA entered the 1960s weakened and riding on Triumph's success. BSA even tried to team up with the former AMC empire in 1972 to form a new company, Norton-Villiers-Triumph, but even that couldn't save it, or Ariel, or the British motorcycle industry as a whole.

Chapter 11
BSA Motorcycles

When BSA Ruled the World
From the mid-1930s to the early-1960s, BSA was the world's largest producer of motorcycles. It owned Triumph, Ariel, Sunbeam and New Hudson Motorcycles, along with factories that made steel, built cars, buses, heavy construction equipment, agricultural and industrial power plants, machine tools, weapons, ammunition, military equipment, bicycles and it even had its own steel mill. It was a bona fide industrial giant, capable of accomplishing almost anything and in far better financial shape than just about any other company in the motorcycle business at that time. By 1960, the BSA Gold Star was a huge hit, on the track and in showrooms, and BSA's A7 (500) and A10 (650) non-unit twins were solid sellers with an excellent reputation. The tiny 2-stroke Bantam was selling like hotcakes, but by 1972, BSA was broke, out of business and irrelevant as a motorcycle company. What happened?

Swords to Ploughshares
BSA started out as a loose alliance of 16 small craftsmen shops in the Coventry area, which teamed up to produce rifles for the British Army during the Crimean War (1853–56), in the days when firearms were painstakingly handcrafted by artisans. It soon realised that two things would be needed for its survival: modern production techniques and a broader product line. By 1884, it was building bicycles, a new thing at the time and all the rage. From there it graduated up to motorised bicycles, then true

This 1929 BSA S29 Twin Port shows why this bike was nicknamed 'Sloper' – because of the pronounced angle of its cylinder.

motorcycles by 1905. At a time when most motorcycle manufacturers were 'cottage industries' that relied on parts brought in from elsewhere (ie engines, gearboxes, etc), BSA was already so big that it was making virtually everything for its bikes in-house.

War and the Post-war Market

World War One was good for BSA. Not only did it sell lots of motorcycles to the British Army, but also by the war's end it was producing 10,000 Lee-Enfield .303 rifles per week! It also built 145,000 Lewis guns. After the war, BSA went back to building reliable, workhorse motorcycles, not necessarily the fastest or the sexiest. It introduced a new OHV 493cc single called the 'Sloper' (because of the sloped angle of the cylinder) in 1926. It developed a line of V- twins to serve the burgeoning sidecar market and continued to refine its big singles, including a new 500cc in 1937, called the Empire Star, which morphed into the legendary BSA Gold Star.

This 1956 BSA DBD34 Gold Star 500 was obviously the street version. However, 'Goldies' also ruled off-road competitions of every type as well as road racing, well into the early 1960s.

This 1948 A7 was one the earliest of BSA's 500cc entry-level twin. It's a good representation of what it was building in the late 1940s.

BSA Gold Star

The 'Goldie' was an instant hit, on the streets, off-road, on racetracks and in showrooms. The big, all-alloy pushrod single was advanced for its day, robust and very fast. Gold Stars were special from the start; every engine was hand-built, then dyno-tested, with the printed results included with every brand-new bike. By the time production ended in 1963, the Gold Star had dominated road racing in Europe and scrambles, desert/off-road racing and even motocross in the US for well over a decade. The dawn of the lightweight 2-stroke spelled the end of the Gold Star's relevance as a dirt bike. Unlike Triumph, which managed the switch in 1963 to unit construction, BSA didn't do nearly as well. The Gold Star was one of the casualties.

BSA Gets a Vertical Twin

When Triumph introduced its seminal 500 Speed Twin in 1937, it set the motorcycle industry on fire, and most manufacturers rushed to develop their own vertical twins. However, World War Two put it all on hold. Not bad for BSA though, which not only sold 130,000 M20 side-valve bikes to the Army, it was back to churning out endless Lee-Enfield rifles, plus (at its peak) 16,390 Browning machine guns per month!

When civilian production resumed in 1946, BSA introduced its own 500 vertical twin, the A7, followed four years later by an 'enlarged' 650cc version called the A10. Both were handsome machines that performed well and were in huge demand until they were replaced by the A50 and A65 in 1962. This was indeed BSA's Golden Age.

Industrial Giant

BSA acquired Ariel in 1944, then Triumph in 1951, both from Jack Sangster who came along with the deal. He sat on BSA's board of directors until the early 1960s and oversaw the stripping and selling-off

The 1970 A65 Lightning 650 was perhaps the ultimate BSA twin, its twin-carburettor answer to the 'Bonneville'. This was the last year before the switch to oil-in-frame.

of BSA's assets. By the time he retired, the once mighty industrial giant was a pitiful shadow of its former self. Not only were the money and all the assets gone, but much of the talent had left also. As a result, BSA made a string of blunders in the 1960s that hastened its trip to the grave.

The 1960s Weren't Good to BSA

In 1962, BSA re-engineered its entire line of twins, replacing the highly successful non-unit construction A7 and A10 with the ungainly, but unit-construction A50 (500) and A65 (650) twins. They weren't nearly as pretty as the bikes they replaced and never really sold as well. The once-elegant engines lost some of their rugged handsomeness, perhaps to their detriment, depending upon ones tastes. BSA applied the same treatment to the Gold Star line with similar results. Sales just got worse and worse. Triumphs, however, were flying off the shelves, especially in America. BSA owned Triumph and should have been celebrating, but instead it resented Triumph's success and treated the company poorly. Business went from bad to worse. What to do? The brilliant minds at BSA decided the answer was a new multi-million-pound research centre in a lavish English country estate called Umberslade Hall.

Not only could BSA not afford it, but Umberslade produced almost nothing of value. A 350 twin that was never produced and the reviled 'oil-bearing frames' introduced on 1971 BSA and Triumph twins were examples of the inept thinking within the elegant walls of Umberslade Hall. Instead of fixing the vibration, oil leaks, shoddy electrics and poor reliability, they chose to build a new frame. They never actually tested it though, so when the new frames hit the production line, they discovered that Triumph's engines wouldn't fit! Really!! The rocker boxes needed to be removed before the engines would slide into place in the frame. Then, the rocker boxes needed to be reinstalled, all on the production line! Thank you, Umberslade Hall.

Left: The pre-1962 non-unit construction BSA A10 had a separate crankcase, primary case and gearbox all bolted together with brackets.

Right: It was replaced by the unit construction A65, with everything packaged in one common casing. BSA called it 'The Power Egg'.

The Switch to Unit Construction

Until this time, most motorcycles had separate engines and gearboxes, connected by a primary chain case, all held together with a system of brackets. This was called non-unit or pre-unit construction. Unit construction consolidated all three components into one unitised casing, hence the name.

Unit construction was all the rage in Britain in the late 1950s. Triumph was the first of the major players to switch, with the 1959 3T 350 twin, and it quickly spread to the 5T 500 twins. Triumph didn't switch the 650 twins out until the 1963 model year. This made only some sense, as all the twins (500 and 650) shared the same architecture in the pre-unit days. The 500 was stretched into a 650 in 1950, but the new unit-construction twins would now split into two distinctly different engine

When introduced in 1969, the BSA Rocket 3 750 triple was fast, but homely. Check out the 'shoebox gas tank' and those crazy 'ray gun' mufflers!

families: the 350 and 500 twins, and the large 650s. Triumph did a good job of styling these new engines to remain faithful to the look it had established with their non-unit engines. Both were clearly Triumphs. BSA chose not to follow this logic. Instead, it completely restyled their engines, taking all the curvaceous shape out of it and turning it into an amorphous blob that it called 'The Power Egg'. It managed to make both sides of the engine look the same, very unusual for a motorcycle engine. It surely cost BSA a fortune to make the switch from pre-unit to unit construction. Perhaps it should have chosen, as Triumph did, to remain faithful to its well-established and well-accepted brand character.

The new A50 500cc unit-twin launched in 1962, with the A65 650cc unit-twin one year behind. There was actually some overlap during this time when both unit and non-unit machines were built. The early unit engines had problems with bearings and bushings, but that was sorted out quickly enough, making them pretty good engines, by the standards of the day. Their early reliability issues hurt sales, and the unit-construction twins never really quite sold as well as the pre-unit bikes in the US. Despite all this, throughout most of the 1960s, the BSA 650 was regarded as one of the fastest motorcycles money could buy.

BSA and Triumph Triples

Perhaps the last gasp was the introduction of the BSA Rocket 3 and the Triumph Trident, both 750cc 3-cylinders. Conceived in 1962 by Triumph's Bert Hopwood, the triple used three sets of the BSA/Triumph 250 hardware, and by 1965, prototypes showed great promise. Triumph wanted to come out with the bikes in 1966 as a '67 model, a move that would have changed history. However, stubborn BSA didn't want Triumph to have that much credit, so it slow-walked the project until 1968 when it became known that Honda was bringing out its game-changing 4-cylinder 750cc. BSA then stepped on the gas and rushed the triples to production to try to beat Honda to market. However, BSA insisted that Triumph build a slightly different engine for BSA's triple, so they wouldn't look alike.

The solution: the Trident had vertical cylinders and the Rocket 3's were slanted slightly forward. Who cares, right? But that little change took time and money that BSA didn't have. Alas, they beat the Honda 750 Four to market by only four months, not nearly enough time to establish themselves, and the triples were more expensive than the big Honda, which had an electric starter, 5-speed gearbox, and a front disc brake. Also, at first they were very ugly. BSA had automotive firm Ogle style the bikes, and the result was ghastly! A 'shoebox' gas tank and 'ray gun' mufflers dominated the look. They never sold in great numbers. By 1970, both Triumph and BSA had straightened out the styling issues, and the triples were turning into great motorcycles. They were handsome machines that handled very well, and they were fast.

The Triumph Trident (left) and the BSA Rocket 3 (right) had nearly identical engines, internally, but BSA insisted on a different look and so its cylinders slanted 12-degrees forward, where the Triumph's cylinders were vertical.

BSA redesigned its 650 twins in 1971, at the same time as Triumph. Its big twins both shared the same oil-bearing frame, along with all the new running gear that gave them a more modern look.

In 1969, a Trident out-accelerated the CB750 in a magazine test. Alas, the last BSA Rocket 3 was produced in 1971 as BSA struggled to survive. Tridents continued on the same Small Heath production line that they both shared through the 1975 model year.

BSA's Last Gasp

By 1971, the entire British motorcycle industry was either dead or on life support. BSA merged with the only other British motorcycle company still standing, Norton-Villiers (formerly AMC) in an attempt to gain some strength. It didn't work. The last BSA motorcycle was built in 1972. Norton continued to build Commandos (now its only model) until 1975. Norton now owned Triumph and tried to shut Triumph's hallowed Meriden factory complex to move Triumph production to Norton's own factory in Donington Park, a move intended to trim costs. Triumph's factory workers revolted in 1974, blockaded themselves inside for nearly a year until a settlement was reached forming the Meriden Co-op, a worker-owned company. It was undercapitalised from the start and struggled on, producing low numbers of Bonnevilles (now its only model) until 1983. Today, BSA is still in business, producing air rifles, rifle scopes and optical equipment.

BSA Update

In 2016, the BSA brand was purchased by Mahindra, the world's largest producer of tractors, with plans to produce new BSA motorcycles in India by 2019. They were to be sold in Europe and the US as premium

motorcycles, possibly retro. However, 2019 came and went, and still no new BSAs. Mahindra, which also bought the Jawa brand and has had nagging production problems trying to launch that bike, has signalled that it regrets getting into the motorcycle business. So, the release of a modern BSA is on hold, at least for now.

This 1971 BSA Gold Star 500SS typified BSA's big singles. They were still considered competitive by some; they were certainly fast and handled well. These were some of the last bikes built by BSA before it shut its doors.

Chapter 12
Matchless Motorcycles

It Started with Bicycles

Established by Henry Herbert Collier as 'Collier & Sons', with sons Charlie and Henry, Matchless Motorcycles started out making bicycles, as did so many other makers of classic British motorcycles. It built its first prototype motorcycle in 1899 and had it in production by 1901. In 1905 it produced a JAP* V-twin powered bike with one of the earliest versions of rear swing arm suspension in motorcycle history. (*JAP was a British company that built engines that were purchased by other manufacturers for their own motorcycles.)

The 498cc 1934 Matchless D80 Sport came out at the tail end of the 'Sloper'-era. It lasted just three model years. From then on, British motorcycles would have vertical cylinders.

AJS engines (left) had its magnetos in front of the cylinder, while Matchless engines (right) placed its behind. Otherwise, they were mechanically identical.

The Early Years

Then they started racing. In 1907, son Charlie won the Inaugural TT Singles Race at an average speed of 38.21mph (blistering speed at the time). His brother, Harry, won in 1909 and Charlie won again in 1910. At the time, they were building mostly singles, with a few V-twins for sidecar duty. Until this point, Matchless Motorcycles were built using other manufacturers' engines, but starting in 1912, Matchless began building its own engines. World War One came and went without them landing any military contracts to build motorcycles for the War Department, but in 1919, production resumed with Matchless building a new V-twin and in 1923, a new single. The father died in 1926, leaving a vibrant family-run business behind. In 1930, Charlie designed a narrow-angle (26 degrees) 400cc V-twin, the Matchless Silver Arrow. This was expanded into a 600cc V-4 in 1931.

Matchless Buys AJS

Also in 1931, Matchless bought AJS Motorcycles from the Stevens brothers, then in the late 1930s bought Sunbeam Motorcycles also, which it would later sell to BSA in 1943. From this point on, all Matchless and AJS Motorcycles would be, mechanically, nearly identical, with slightly different styling. The only major mechanical difference between the two was that Matchless positioned the magneto behind the cylinder, and the AJS had its magneto in front of the cylinder. Otherwise, they were essentially the same machines built on the same production line. Each had its own model designation. The Matchless G80 (500 single) became the AJS Model 18. The Matchless G9 (500 twin) was the AJS Model 20, and so on.

A Supplier of Engines

In 1933, Matchless began supplying V-twin engines to the Morgan Car Company for its cute, little, 3-wheeled cars and became the exclusive supplier by 1935. From 1935 to 1940, Matchless V-twins were supplied to Brough Superior for all its motorcycles (this is the bike that Lawrence of Arabia rode). In 1935, Matchless engineers invented the 'hairpin' valve springs that would become a trademark of the two brands.

Matchless supplied V-twin engines to the Morgan Car Company for its cute 3-wheeled cars.

The Fred Loudon motorcycle dealership sold Francis-Barnett motorcycles on the corner of Elizabeth and Goulburn Streets in London. This photo was taken in 1938.

AMC is Born

In 1938, Associated Motor Cycles (AMC) was formed, to hold a stable of brands that included not only Matchless and AJS, but also Sunbeam, James, Francis-Barnett and, ultimately, Norton Motorcycles.

War Intervenes

In 1941, Matchless and AJS introduced what is regarded as the first truly telescopic front fork, called 'Teledraulic', to rave reviews. World War Two saw Matchless build 80,000 G3 and G3L 350cc singles for the British military. Its post-war singles were based on the wartime Matchless G3L. 1949 saw the company's first vertical twin, the 500cc Matchless G9 (and the AJS Model 20). In 1956 it was enlarged to 600cc (G12 and AJS Model 31) and in 1959 to 650cc (G15 and AJS Model 33).

The quintessential Matchless: a 1948 G80 500cc single.

Post-war Racing

In racing, the supercharged AJS Porcupine, Matchless G50 and AJS 7R were winning races and helping to cement the reputations of Matchless and AJS as fast, dependable machines. In 1952, Derek Farrant won the Manx GP on a 1952 Matchless G45 twin averaging 88.65mph. AMC withdrew from racing at the end of the 1954 season, concentrating on sales. However, unlike most manufacturers, Matchless and AJS were selling pretty much the same race bikes to the public that the factory had fielded, and their sales of race bikes continued long after the factory stopped racing. The 1959 Matchless G50 500cc single, for instance, had 50 horsepower, would do 135mph and was faster than a Norton Manx. When Bert Hopwood left AMC for Triumph in 1961, some of the racing magic faded.

Matchless and AJS had to join the vertical twin race like almost everyone else. In 1949 they jumped in with both feet with the 500cc G9. This is a 1951 Matchless G9. The AJS version was called the Model 20.

Matchless and AJS have Twins!

Following the example of nearly every other British motorcycle manufacturer, Matchless needed a vertical twin to compete with the Triumph, BSA and Norton twins. AMC felt it should improve upon Triumph's design, and so used a centre main bearing on the crankshaft, which added immense strength and rigidity when compared to the deflection-prone cranks in the Triumph and every other

This 1968 Matchless G80CS (500 single) was the ultimate evolution of AMC singles.

British vertical twin that followed. All except the Matchless and AJS twins had only the two outer main bearings with a huge central flywheel supported only by the rod journals. This 3-bearing set-up allowed AMC to make the one-piece crank out of a heavy-duty cast iron, instead of steel.

As was their custom, two versions of the bike were built, one for Matchless and one for AJS. Both were nearly mechanically identical, with some styling differences. The 500cc Matchless G9 (and AJS Model 20) launched in 1949. It was punched out to 648cc in 1958 with the Matchless G12 and AJS Model 31, and in 1961 they bored and stroked it out to 750cc for the Matchless G15 and the AJS Model 33. There were also racing versions that did very well in road racing at the time.

Hard Times

By 1960, the writing was on the wall: sales were down, and the future looked bleak for AMC. Between its five once-proud brands: Matchless, AJS, James, Francis-Barnett and Norton, only Norton was actually making money. The decision was made to drop everything but the Matchless/AJS singles and focus everything else on Norton Motorcycles. The singles didn't sell as well in the 1960s; even Norton sales weren't as strong as hoped, and by 1966, AMC was bankrupt. Manganese Bronze Holdings (which also owned Villiers Motorcycles) bought it out, forming a new company, Norton-Villiers, with ambitious plans to become big players in the British motorcycle industry. It planned to do this with one motorcycle: the Norton Commando. The rest is history. As for Matchless and AJS, a few 1967s were sold, and some unsold bikes were retagged as 1968s and licensing deals produced a few more Matchless-badged bikes scattered here and there, most notably on the Rotax-engined Les Harris Matchless G80 in 1988. Alas, by the close of the 1960s, Matchless and AJS were added to the scrapheap that was once the proud British motorcycle industry. Truly a pity.

After AMC's collapse, Norton-Villiers owned the rights to AJS. However, by this time, AJS and Matchless 4-stroke singles were no longer competitive with lighter, more powerful 2-strokes, so they built their own 2-stroke with a Villiers 250cc engine. This one's a 1970 AJS Stormer motocrosser.

Chapter 13
Norton Motorcycles

Norton, Always a Game Changer

James Lansdowne Norton began building motorcycles in 1902 using French and Swiss engines. By 1907, he was building his own and winning races with them, including the first ever Isle of Man TT. This began a racing heritage that is the stuff of legend. Today, Nortons are among the most popular, fastest, best-handling and sexiest of all classic British motorcycles. The Norton Commando (1969–75) was considered by many to be the world's first production superbike; it actually *was* the world's fastest production motorcycle at the time of its introduction in 1968 and one of the most desirable machines of all time. It represented the best that the British motorcycle industry had to offer at the time. It was a genuine game-changer, but game-changers were nothing new to Norton. Its 350 and 500 Manx singles were lightyears ahead of the competition at the time and dominated road racing for decades.

This 1949 Norton Manx had advanced features like a twin-leading shoe front brake, a DOHC engine, tuned-exhaust megaphone and the 'Featherbed' frame.

Norton Manx

The Manx is a breed of cat that is born with no tail and is native to the Isle of Man, a small island off the coast of England that is the scene of one of the oldest and greatest of all motorcycle races, the Manx GP. The Manx motorcycle launched in 1938 and was typical of Norton's obsession with mechanical perfection, with DOHCs driven by a shaft-and-bevel-gear set-up. By 1950, when most motorcycles still used rigid frames (no rear suspension), Norton introduced the revolutionary 'Featherbed' frame that set the pattern for nearly every motorcycle frame built for the next 30 years. The Featherbed (so-named because of its smooth ride) used a conventional swing arm, novel in 1950, and all-welded steel tubing, at a time when most frames were held together with heavy brazed lugs. Additionally, the frame tubes were triangulated to distribute the loads placed on the steering head and swingarm pivot, making them immensely strong and rigid, and yet light.

This 1959 Manx had shaft-driven DOHCs, with exposed 'hairpin' valve springs no less, a heavily finned all-alloy top end, a Lucas magneto and an Amal GP carburettor.

This 1951 Norton ES2 is a good example of Norton's big street bikes of the day. A long-stroke 500cc OHV single with a cast-iron top end and plunger rear suspension. The Manx got all the good stuff.

This lightness and rigidity caused the Manx to handle better than anything else on the road or the track in its day. This handling advantage proved pivotal in its racing career, as the Norton Manx dominated Grand Prix racing and the Isle of Man TT well into the 1960s. However, it wasn't just the good handling of the Featherbed frame that gave the Manx its edge. It was fast, very fast. The 350cc or 500cc single-cylinder engines were DOHC at a time when most bikes still had pushrods, and some of their contemporaries were still using side-valve arrangements (flatheads). However, the days of the single-cylinder British bike were numbered.

When Big Singles Ruled the World

The British motorcycle industry in the 1930s was dominated by OHV air-cooled single-cylinder designs, all very similar in layout. Every major British brand had one, some had several. Over many years, they slowly expanded these engines in both displacement and output, until by the late 1930s, they had very nearly reached their physical limits at about 500cc and 30 horsepower. Any increase in either number led to excessive vibration.

Norton joined the vertical twin race in 1949 with its 500cc Model 7. This is a 1952 Norton Model 7. Note the plunger rear suspension.

The Modern Twin is Born

In 1938, Edward Turner, legendary designer of the Ariel Square Four engine, devised a radical new approach to the vibration problem in the parallel twin, launched in the new Triumph 500 Speed Twin. Part of its genius was that it used the same technology and tooling as Triumph's singles, making it easier and cheaper to produce. It used two smaller pistons rather than one large one to make up its 500cc of displacement, both rising and falling together, but firing alternately. They were much smoother than the big singles of similar displacement, and they loved to rev. It was a stroke of genius and it revolutionised the motorcycle industry overnight. Alas, World War Two started a year later, ending production until 1946. However, when civilian motorcycle production ramped back up after the war, every British manufacturer wanted their own 500cc parallel twin, including Norton. In 1949 Norton launched its first twin, the 500cc Model 7. Development continued unabated as it built successively larger and more powerful twin-cylinder machines, all from this original architecture. In fact, this little 500cc twin became the basis for every motorcycle it built from the mid-1960s on, until its demise in 1975, by which time it had been pushed all the way out to 850cc.

Following the 500cc Model 7, the Dominator series stretched the little 500cc to 600cc, then 650cc. This is a 650cc 1959 Norton Dominator 99. Besides the boost in power, what made the Dominator dominate was the Featherbed frame. It's easy to spot as it has a gently curved frame tube that runs from the swingarm pivot to the back of the tank.

Norton Dominator

Norton mounted the Model 7's 500 twin-cylinder into the Manx's new Featherbed frame in 1953, and named the new bike the Dominator 88. It ran through 1963, during which time Norton bored it out to 600cc, creating the Dominator 99. In 1962, Norton punched it out again, this time to 650cc, renaming it the Dominator 650SS, which ran through 1969, overlapping Commando production by a year.

The Atlas was the next evolution in Norton twins, stretching it out still further to 750cc. It was fast and handled extremely well, as did everything that used the vaunted Featherbed. As power increased, vibration started to be a problem.

Norton Atlas: Horsepower Wars

The race was on for bigger engines and more power. Triumph had enlarged its own 500 twin to 650cc in 1950 and was continually hopping it up further, first with the T110 Tiger in 1953, then the TR6 in 1956, and then with the legendary twin-carburettor Bonneville in 1959. Norton had to step up its game. So, in 1962, it bored out the engine again, this time to 750cc, juicing up the styling a bit, and the Norton Atlas was born. By this time, the vertical twin in general was also reaching its physical limits, and the Norton twin, now making 55 horsepower, was no exception. Vibration was always a factor in parallel twins, with both pistons rising and falling together, and it was only getting worse: the larger those pistons got, the more power they made and the faster the engines turned.

The ultimate evolution of the Dominator was the 650SS, still with Featherbed frame, but more power. This is a 1969 Norton Dominator 650SS.

Vibration is the New Enemy

Triumph, BSA and all the other British motorcycle manufacturers were experiencing the same vibration problems and needed a solution. The long-term answer would have been to design completely new, totally modern engines, more like the Japanese models. However, the much lower-volume British were perpetually strapped for cash and simply couldn't afford it. Finances forced Norton, Triumph, BSA and the rest of the British firms to make do with the engines they had, so Norton, true to its tradition of innovation, approached the vibration problem from a totally new direction. It created yet another iconic motorcycle frame, this one with what it called 'isolastic suspension', which rubber mounted the engine in common with the swing arm to isolate the engine's vibration and channel it out the rear wheel to the road. It was brilliant and proved to be highly effective at quelling the big Norton's otherwise wicked engine vibration.

The Commando mounted the engine at a forward slant to give it a more modern look. Isolastic suspension damped the vibes, allowing Norton to extract more power from the engine, and it was fast. The engine package was rubber mounted in the frame, in common with the swingarm. This is a 1971 Norton Commando Roadster.

The Norton Commando is Born

The new frame bequeathed a new bike, the 750cc 1969 Norton Commando, arguably Norton's most famous bike, certainly its biggest commercial success. The Commando was an instant hit. It was a handsome machine, fast and powerful; it handled well, and it was smooth, very smooth. At the time of its launch, more than a full year ahead of the Honda 750 Four and the Triumph Trident, the Commando was considered to be the world's fastest production motorcycle and is considered by some to be the world's first 'superbike'.

The Commando was a handsome brute, with loads of power, great handling and a smoothness previously unknown to British twins. For a brief time the Commando was known as the 'World's Fastest Motorcycle'. Then the Trident came out, then the Honda CB750. This is a 1971 Norton Commando Roadster with a custom Corbin seat.

One Step Forward, Two Steps Back

The Commando came in a variety of body styles: Roadster (the standard), Fastback (styler) and Interstate (touring version). Norton seemed adept at spinning off 'special models' like the Production Racer and the John Player Norton (part of a cross-promotion with the famous British cigarette maker), by hanging trick bodywork on an otherwise stock Commando. It may have overreached, however, with the 'Hi-Rider', its hideous attempt at a factory chopper. Over the next few years, evolutionary changes were made, including punching it out again to 850cc and adding a front disc brake in 1973 and an electric starter in 1975. This, the same engine that started

The 1974–75 John Player Norton, or JPN, was a special limited-edition factory cafe racer commemorating Norton's road racing wins with the sponsorship of the British cigarette maker John Player. Underneath all the dressing was a stock 850 Commando. This one is a 1974 model.

life as a 500cc twin! But the extra displacement allowed the power to come on at a lower rpm, making the bike smoother and a better overall road machine. Ultimate performance was becoming irrelevant in old British bikes like the Norton and the Triumph, in the face of the onslaught of modern superbikes from Japan. You didn't buy a British bike to be the fastest, so what motivated buyers to buy Nortons? Who knows, but by 1975, the company wasn't selling enough Commandos to keep the doors open, and production ended.

The Death of the British Motorcycle Industry

Alas, the writing was on the wall. The entire British motorcycle industry, once the envy of the world, was a hollowed-out shell of its former self by the end of the 1960s. The few left standing struggled at the edge of insolvency. A British government hostile to industry was part of the problem. Unbelievably bad management by those making the business decisions was another part of it, a very big part, but they were also victims of changing times. The world was turning a corner, away from cottage industries manned by artisans hand-making antiquated products in low volumes and towards the modern high-tech model typified by the Japanese. The British industry was artisan-based and very traditional. Continual improvements were made year by year to the same old designs, which were produced in the same way they had been for decades. The Japanese held no such loyalty to their past, embracing anything that would help them make more bikes, better, cheaper and faster. They literally swamped the British bike industry on a scale that the British could never have competed with.

Norton attempted to revive its chances during the 1980s and once again led the way with a series of twin-rotor Wankel-powered bikes. Only a few hundred were built. Overheating problems plagued the bike from the start. This is a 1988 Norton P43 Classic Rotary.

This 2010 Norton 961 Commando is a totally modern bike yet instantly recognisable as a Norton Commando. Unfortunately, they're built in such low numbers that you rarely see one.

The Last Gasp

BSA, which in 1960 was the world's largest producer of motorcycles and one of the largest multinational corporations overall, by 1972 was broke and out of business, and it owned Triumph. Norton-Villiers, the only other British company still standing, merged with BSA, which owned Triumph. BSA folded and Norton ended up with Triumph. In early 1974, Norton announced that it would be closing Triumph's Meriden plant and moving Triumph production to Norton's own factories in Donington, to save on costs. The Triumph workers revolted, barricaded themselves in the factory and didn't come out until a deal was struck in 1975 to form the worker-owned Meriden Co-op. Norton itself was struggling to stay alive, but the last Norton Commando rolled off the assembly line in 1975 (although some of the unsold bikes were retitled as '76s and '77s). Triumph, now owned by its workers, struggled along until 1983.

The Modern Norton

Several attempts have been made to revive the hallowed Norton name, including the stillborn 1987 Norton twin-rotor Wankel motorcycle. American Kenny Dreer bought the rights to the Commando in the 1990s, and designed and hand-built new 961 Commandos in Oregon, in very small numbers. In 2006, UK businessman Stuart Garner, owner of Norton Racing Ltd, acquired the rights to the Norton Commando brand. He had a totally new bike designed from a clean sheet of paper, using modern technology but meant it to be instantly recognisable as a Commando. The Norton 961 Commando launched in 2010 and is still in limited production today.

Chapter 14

Royal Enfield Motorcycles

The Early Days

Royal Enfield motorcycles were never one of the top sellers among the classic British motorcycle brands, but they were known to be fast, rugged and often unique and interesting. Like so many British motorcycle companies at the time, Royal Enfield started out making bicycles in 1893 as the Enfield Manufacturing Company Ltd. By 1899, it had built its first quadracycle with a De Dion engine. It added 'Royal' to the Enfield name, and in 1912 started racing with its Royal Enfield Model 80, powered by a 770cc JAP V-twin, enjoying some success at the Isle of Man TT and Brooklands.

The sidecar market was big in the 1930s. This 1939 Royal Enfield Model H was designed for sidecar duty, with its torquey 570cc side-valve single.

World War One and After

World War One brought rich contracts from both the British War Department and Imperial Russia for three different models: a 225cc two-stroke, a 425cc V-twin and an 8hp sidecar rig with a Vickers machine gun mounted on it. With the end of the war, Royal Enfield concentrated on the civilian market with a new 976cc V-twin in 1921 and its first 4-stroke single, albeit with a JAP 350cc engine. In 1928, it added a saddle tank and centre-sprung girder front fork, state-of-the-art for the day, which Royal Enfield was one of the first to adopt.

The 'Flying Flea' was meant to parachute in with British troops during the war, but when peace came, Royal Enfield quickly converted them over to civilian use. The British home market was starved of cheap, economical transportation after the war, and bikes like this sold like hotcakes.

Bikes for World War Two

Despite all this, the company was in dire financial straits, barely limping along. In 1931, one of the founders, Albert Eddie, died. Then, just two years later, his partner, R W Smith, also died. Times were tough, and the Depression had set in, but Royal Enfield somehow managed to keep going. World War Two hit at just the right time, and again it was flooded with lucrative government contracts for a large number of military motorcycles. These included a 250cc side-valve (SV), a 350cc SV, two 350cc OHV singles, a 570cc SV single and the most famous of them all, the Flying Flea. The Flea was a lightweight, rugged 125cc two-stroke that could be parachuted in with airborne troops. To avoid bombing by the Luftwaffe, a brand

The 350cc and 500cc single-cylinder Bullets were always Royal Enfield's bestsellers. This one is a 350cc 1949 G2 Bullet.

new factory was built underground in Westwood, England, where it was found that the constant temperatures were ideal for making not only motorcycles, but also 'predictor' detonators for anti-aircraft artillery shells.

Built in India

After the war, Royal Enfield resumed civilian production with the 350cc OHV Model G single and the 500cc OHV Model J single, both with rigid frames and telescopic forks. In 1948, it unveiled its groundbreaking new swing arm rear suspension, one of the first to do so. By the late 1950s, Royal Enfield was struggling again financially and so sold the non-exclusive licensing and manufacturing rights, and tooling, for the Bullet to Madras Motors in India. Madras commenced production in India of 350cc Royal Enfield Bullets, and later expanded to 500cc Bullet production, all singles. From then on, the British Royal Enfield continued to produce bikes for the UK, Europe and America, while the Indian Royal Enfield built bikes that were sold in India and throughout Asia. All Indian-produced Royal Enfields were single-cylinder bikes until 2018 when the company introduced an all-new 650 twin, in the classic British vertical twin mould (well, almost vertical). Even though the British arm of Royal Enfield is long gone, the Indian arm is still producing bikes to this day, to a huge domestic market within India, a large export market in the developing world and even to Europe and America, where they are viewed as 'retro'. The basic design of the single-cylinder Bullet has changed little since the 1950s, and it shows, even though today the bikes have electric starters and fuel injection. This new 'Indian Enfield' is built in a variety of styles, some mimicking military machines and some 1950s classics.

Indian-built Royal Enfields have a very 'retro' look, despite electric starters and fuel injection. This is a 500cc 2002 Royal Enfield Bullet.

Twins from England

At this point, Royal Enfield was still building bikes itself at its Bradford-on-Avon factory in England. In 1949, it joined the vertical twin race with its own 500cc Royal Enfield Meteor. By 1953, it had punched it out to 700cc (hoping to trump Triumph and BSA, which only had 650s) with the Royal Enfield Super Meteor. It punched it out again in 1962 to 750cc with the Royal Enfield Interceptor, all the while, building lots of 18hp 250cc OHV Royal Enfield Crusaders and Bullets. It also dabbled in two-strokes, like the Villiers-engined 250 Turbo Twin. However, nothing seemed to add up to the sales it needed to survive.

Royal Enfield put great care into the design of its own entry into the vertical twin foray, and it did an excellent job of it. The 750 Interceptor was a fast, robust, handsome machine.

Indian Enfields and Enfield Indians

An interesting twist in the Royal Enfield story is how Super Meteor 700cc twins were rebadged as Indian Motorcycles and sold to the US market as the Indian Chief from 1955 to 1960. Interesting story. Indian had itself changed hands during World War Two, and after the war, the new owners wanted to get out of the heavy V-twin market to embrace the 'new wave' of parallel twins pouring in from Britain. They had tried unsuccessfully to lobby the US government to impose heavy tariffs and limits on British imports. When that failed, they decided that if you can't beat 'em, join 'em. Indian squandered its dwindling resources on trying to build its own vertical twin on the British pattern, but failed miserably. In 1953, bankrupt Indian changed hands again and the new owner, Brockhouse Engineering, also happened to be the exclusive US importer for Royal Enfield Motorcycles. Starting in 1955, it painted Royal Enfield Super Meteors in bright colours, slapped on a huge leather saddle with tassels, along with garish Indian logos. It gave them appropriate names like 'Indian Chief', 'Tomahawk' and 'Hounds Fire Arrow'. Indian Motorcycles had thrown all its eggs into the Royal Enfield basket when it ended decades of production of its own V-twin. Unfortunately, the rebadged 'Enfield Indians' didn't do well and so the marketing agreement was cancelled in 1960, at which point Royal Enfield Motorcycles became available in the US under its own name. So, another oddity is that there are both 'Enfield Indians' and 'Indian Enfields'.

From 1955 to 1960 Royal Enfield 700 Super Meteors were rebadged as Indian Chiefs and given lots of garish details to make them look like Indian Enfields. They didn't do well in America, but paved the way for Royal Enfield's entry into the US market. This is a 1960 Indian Chief.

The Royal Enfield in India had never built anything but singles until 2018 when it launched this stunning new 650 vertical (well, almost vertical) twin. This one is a 2019 Royal Enfield GT650.

The End Draws Near

By the mid-1960s, the horsepower race was raging. The Japanese were on the march, and everyone was pumping up their bikes for more power. Royal Enfield followed suit by punching out the 700cc to 750cc with its Series I and Series II 750 Interceptor, now good for a 13 second quarter mile at 105mph. The US loved the bike, but cash-strapped Royal Enfield was unable to produce them in large enough volumes quickly enough to meet the demand. That, and a reputation for leaking oil (earning it the nickname 'Royal Oilfield'), led to its final slide into insolvency. By 1967, production had stopped, with unsold bikes being retitled all the way out to 1970 and sold as new. The factory was closed for good in 1970, at which time Royal Enfield (the British one, now completely separated from the Indian company) was acquired by Manganese Bronze Holdings and added to the scrap heap that would become Norton-Villiers, which would ultimately include Triumph, BSA, Norton, Matchless/AJS, Ariel, James, Francis-Barnett and now Royal Enfield. Nothing much came of it. Royal Enfield was added to the long list of failed British motorcycle companies.

Three Centuries of Bikes

However, Royal Enfield is the only motorcycle company still building bikes that can claim to have done so over a span of three centuries! It started in the 1800s, ran though the 1900s, and is still producing bikes in 2020. Not even old-timers Triumph Motorcycles (1902) and Harley-Davidson (1903) can make that claim!

Chapter 15
Triumph Motorcycles

In the Beginning

Like most British motorcycle companies of the era, Triumph started out making bicycles. Formed by Siegfried Bettmann (a German, not a Briton) in 1883 as a bicycle maker, by 1902 the company was building motorcycles. It quickly established a reputation for quality and performance. By the onset of World War One, it was well enough established to provide 30,000 motorcycles to the British Army, where it earned the respect of British troops for its reliability in the field, prompting the nickname 'Trusty Triumph'. Throughout the 1920s and 1930s it continued to develop better and more powerful machines.

This 1939 Triumph 3HW 350 represents a fairly typical pre-war single, among Triumph and its contemporaries. A big, strokey OHV single with rigid frame and girder forks.

The 500cc Triumph Speed Twin is credited with starting the whole 'vertical twin-boom' in 1938. Soon nearly every other British bike maker followed suit with their own 500 twins. This is a 1938 Triumph 5T Speed Twin engine.

Big Singles Ruled

By the mid-1930s, virtually the entire industry had settled into one basic engine design that was more or less universal. With few exceptions, everyone was building pushrod-operated (OHV) air-cooled singles with small bores and long strokes (undersquare).

By this time, engine displacement and performance were approaching their practical limits at about 500cc and 30 horsepower. Anything more on either number induced wicked engine vibration. Lots of things were tried, but nothing could counteract the forces of that one big, heavy piston flying around the cylinder at high speed.

The Vertical Twin is Born

Triumph approached the vibration problem from a whole new direction. Engine designer Edward Turner, who also designed the Ariel Square Four, came up with the parallel, or vertical twin, which used two smaller pistons making up 500cc, rising and falling together on a 360-degree crankshaft, but firing alternately. The crank rode on just two main bearings, just like the big singles, which saved on

In 1950, Triumph introduced its first 650 twin, the 6T Thunderbird. This is a 1952. Check out that saddlebag, which the British call a 'pannier'.

tooling costs. The new 500 twin was brought to market as the 1938 Triumph 5T Speed Twin. It was an instant hit. Unfortunately, World War Two started just a year later and civilian production didn't resume until 1946. However, when it did, Speed Twins were selling as fast as Triumph could build them. Joining them in 1946 was a new, hotter version of the 500 twin. With higher compression and wilder cams, the 500cc Triumph T100 Tiger was the hottest thing going at the time.

More Power, Scotty!

But in the motorcycle business, 'too much is never enough'. What's more, Triumph's biggest market was America, and Americans wanted power and lots of it. During the next 20 years or so, Triumph built its reputation on fielding fast, excellent handling, handsome machines that could beat just about anything on the street. To accommodate this growing trend, Triumph added displacement and horsepower. In 1950, it bored and stroked the 500 twin out to 649cc, creating the first Triumph 650, the 1950 6T Thunderbird. Another instant hit, but before long, more power was needed. It applied the 'Tiger treatment' (higher compression and hotter cams) to the new 650 to create the more powerful 1954 T110 Tiger.

Triumph Nomenclature

In Triumph parlance, these alpha-numeric designations are supposed to reference the top speed of the bike. Thus, in theory, a 500cc T100 was good for 100mph, and so the larger, faster 650cc version must then be able to hit 110, hence the T110 moniker. The Bonneville came later and was faster still, so it became the T120. When Triumph punched out the Bonneville to 750cc in 1973, it became the T140. Could it really do 140mph? I doubt it. Since the Trident triple was Triumph's fastest bike, clearly it had to be a T150, and in its final year, the redesigned 1975 Trident became the T160. How many people hit 160mph on their classic Trident? However, this naming convention worked for Triumph, and for the buying public, although most of them referred to their Triumphs by their sexy-sounding model names, such as Bonneville, Tiger or Trident. Very few used the alpha-numeric designations to describe their bikes.

During the late 1940s and early 1950s, the fastest bike on the road was the Triumph T110 Tiger. Tuning secrets learned in racing were applied to the pedestrian 6T Thunderbird engine to give them more power. This is a 650cc 1955 Triumph T110 Tiger.

The 1956 TR6 introduced the alloy Delta head and even more power. This is actually a 1957 TR6 Trophy, which was the off-road version with high pipe and knobby tyres. The TR6 Tiger was the street version.

More Power – Again!

This was soon followed up by yet a faster version in 1956 called the TR6 Trophy, sporting a new alloy cylinder head called the 'Delta head' that offered improved cooling and flowed better for even more power. The TR6 not only had a more powerful engine, but it was stripped down for off-road or desert racing, although street versions still had lights. The TR6 had a smaller, shapelier 'teardrop' tank and bodywork, better seats and trim and slim fenders, compared to the Thunderbirds and Tigers with their stodgy headlight nacelles and full-valance mudguards. During this time, Triumphs were not only winning in the showroom, they were dominating road racing, off-road scrambles and particularly desert racing, which evolved into motocross.

The Bonneville is Born

Regardless, more power was needed, so, in 1959, Triumph reworked the Delta head and mounted two carburettors on it and created a whole new bike, the 1959 T120 Bonneville. At the time, nearly every twin was running a single carburettor. It looks like an obvious improvement now, but it was revolutionary at the time and boosted the Bonneville's image even more than its actual performance. The twin carburettors helped mostly at high RPMs but didn't add much in traffic, and they proved fussy to tune. However, these seemed irrelevant issues as the public perception was that the new 650 Bonneville was THE fastest thing around, on two or four wheels.

Despite being the 'baddest' motorcycle on the planet in 1959, the Bonneville launched with the stodgy headlight nacelle and full-valance fenders, along with the fuddy-duddy seat from the plebian Thunderbird. That and the orange and cream paint scheme made it look dull. Instead of styling it like the bad boy it was, it made it look like an old man's bike. However, it didn't take Triumph long to catch on. By 1960, they were styled just like the svelte TR6.

Clunky Styling

Triumph, however, usually a styling leader, totally missed the mark when styling the 1959 Bonneville. It came clad in the clunky 'old-man' bodywork from the Thunderbird and Tiger, with its old-fashioned headlight nacelle and massive full-valance mudguards, all in an odd 2-tone paint job of orange and cream. The most 'macho' bike on the planet at the time, performance-wise, looked like an old fuddy-duddy. Many a buyer had the dealers install the more attractive TR6 bodywork on their new Bonnevilles before picking them up. However, Triumph wasted no time in correcting that gaffe. From 1960 on, the Bonneville was styled like the TR6, but with its own unique paint scheme, which changed every model year.

Note the racier styling of the 1962 Triumph Bonneville. This was the last year before the switch to new unit construction.

Unit Construction

The next major change in the Triumph lineage started in 1959 with the new 350 and 500 Triumph twins. It spread to the 650 line in 1963 with the adoption of 'unit construction'. Triumph 650 twins built prior to this are called 'pre-unit' or 'non-unit' bikes, which signifies that the engine, the primary chain case, and the gearbox were all separate components that were bolted together with a system of brackets. In 1963, all of these components were incorporated into one integrated casing (in two halves), as one 'unit', hence the name 'unit construction'. This enabled a lighter, more compact engine package that was easier and cheaper to assemble, had fewer maintenance and repair problems, was quieter, cleaner and stronger. Strong enough hopefully to withstand the next wave of horsepower enhancements.

Above left: Through 1962, pre-unit twins had separate engines, primary cases and gearboxes.

Above right: From 1963 on, unit-construction twins incorporated everything into one unitised casing.

This 1965 T120R Bonneville represents Triumph and the Bonneville at their peak. They had virtually no competition at this point, but the Japanese were coming. By 1965, the first Honda 'Black Bomber' DOHC 450s came out, offering up the first real challenge to the Bonneville's dominance.

Triumph's Heyday

The 1960s were Triumph's heyday, and the Bonneville and TR6 led the way. Faster than just about any other motorcycles on the road and quicker than most cars, the Bonneville took on a mystique and an icon-status that was bigger than life. If you wanted to be cool back in 1965, you rode a Bonneville. Sales were peaking, and every year Triumph made improvements and refinements to all their bikes, so that by 1970, the Triumph 650 twin, both Bonneville and TR6, had probably reached their zenith. Half a world away in Japan, they'd just entered the heavyweight, high-performance motorcycle game in a very big way with a major financial and technical achievement that immediately produced results like the Honda 750 Four and Kawasaki's insane 500cc Mach III two-stroke triple – and they were just getting started. At this same time, the entire British motorcycle industry was going belly up. BSA, which in 1960 was the world's largest producer of motorcycles and one of the biggest multinational corporations on Earth, by 1970 was broke. Bad management, an unfriendly socialist government and changing times would have probably done them in anyway. However, BSA's arrogance and hubris finished the company off. During the 1960s, as Triumph was breaking sales records every year, parent company BSA should have been celebrating, but instead it actually resented Triumph's success and often worked against Triumph out of some perverse sense of company pride. Back in Britain, BSAs were still popular enough, but in the all-important US market, BSA's sales were down, and its sales star, Triumph, was getting far less support than it should have, all things considered. In the end, all that bad behaviour came home to roost. BSA was soon finished, survived by Triumph.

Changes were Coming

However, by this time, Honda, Yamaha, Kawasaki and Suzuki were flooding the market with cheap, reliable bikes that were getting faster and better every year. By 1970, Honda was building more bikes

When first introduced, the 1969 Triumph Trident and BSA Rocket 3 both came with ungainly 'shoebox' gas tanks and 'ray gun' mufflers, also known as 'Flash Gordons'. Who would style a bike like this? The geniuses at BSA hired an automotive supplier called Ogle to create this masterpiece. By late 1969, they were adopting normal Bonneville-derived bodywork.

in one month than the entire British motorcycle industry built in a year. The poor British just couldn't compete, and they weren't willing to change. Of course, they were perpetually strapped for cash, so big changes weren't necessarily an option. However, it's clear that the British intended to continue building the same Triumphs, BSAs and Nortons they always had, in pretty much the same way, just improving them year-by-year. Meanwhile, the Japanese were embracing all the latest manufacturing techniques, anything that would increase production volume, and their bikes were getting faster every year, and bigger. The final death blow was the introduction of the seminal 1969 Honda CB750 Four. Triumph and BSA managed to beat the mighty Honda to market by a few months with their own multi-cylinder super bikes, the Triumph 750 Trident and the BSA 750 Rocket 3, both with three cylinders.

Trident Triple

Back in 1962, having just moved from Matchless to Triumph, Bert Hopwood came up with the idea of coupling three BSA/Triumph 250 singles into a 750cc triple, and by 1965 they were testing the prototype. Triumph wanted to introduce the bike in 1966 as a 1967 model, to be named the T150 Trident, a move that would have changed history. It would have beat the Honda to market by two full years and established itself as THE superbike. The first mainstream 3-cylinder. It could have changed the world's perception of what a British motorcycle was. However, proud BSA, unwilling to give that much credit to Triumph, dragged its feet until the Triumph engineers could come up with a BSA version of the new bike. Additionally, BSA wouldn't settle for rebadging the Trident, which would have been the smart move. It wanted a unique version with a different-looking engine.

While the Trident had vertical cylinders, the new BSA Rocket 3 was to have its cylinders canted slightly forward (at 12 degrees) with different outer covers that looked more 'BSA-like'. These changes required entirely new engine castings, which increased costs and delayed introduction

Left: The Triumph Trident engine had vertical cylinders.

Right: The BSA Rocket 3's cylinders slant forward 12 degrees. This required new bottom end cases and covers, on otherwise identical engines.

The 1971 Triumph T150 Trident benefited from all the new bodywork and running gear from the 1971 Oil-in-Frame twins. Despite early teething problems, the big Triple turned into an incredible machine for the times and a brilliant achievement for the cash-strapped British firm.

until 1968 (as 1969 models), just weeks before Honda's game-changing CB750 hit the market. While they were fast, when introduced they were both hideous wretches. Clever BSA had hired an automotive firm called Ogle to style the bikes. It decided that boxy gas tanks and mufflers that looked like Flash Gordon's ray gun would make them look modern. The looks were a joke, and by 1970 they'd restyled the Trident to look more like the handsome Bonnevilles. Once they worked the bugs out, the Trident was a great machine: fast, with good handling, comfortable to ride and oh so handsome.

The ultimate Triumph Triple didn't start out as a Triumph. The 1973 Triumph X-75 Hurricane was originally intended to be a BSA. Hence the BSA Rocket 3 engine and frame. However, BSA folded in 1972, and Triumph inherited the project. Some quick restyling and voila! Alas, it lasted just one year with barely 1,000 built.

They were actually a little quicker than a CB750 and easily out-handled them. However, because of the currency exchange rate at the time, the Trident cost more than the CB750, and the Honda came with an electric starter, a 5-speed gearbox and a front disc brake. Best of all, the Honda started every time; the lights always worked; it was totally reliable and never, never leaked oil. The poor Trident was hopelessly outclassed.

BSA Bungling

All British bikes, including Triumph's entire line-up, were suddenly outclassed. The Bonneville, already making around 50 horsepower, couldn't be pushed much further without suffering wicked vibration and reliability problems. Parent company BSA, in its infinite wisdom, became famous during this period for its total ineptness and stupidity. For the 1971 model year, BSA spent millions developing new frames for BSA and Triumph 650 twins. Saddled with antiquated

The 1971 Triumph T120 Bonneville was a very handsome machine, yet when they came out, they were actually reviled by traditionalists for their looks.

engines, oil leakage problems, vibration problems, sketchy electrics and a growing reputation for poor reliability, BSA put its money into a new frame (which was already one of the industry's best), not new engines or better electrics. These new frames carried their oil inside the backbone of the frame itself, rather than in a separate oil tank. Because of this, Triumph and BSA 650 and 750 twins, from 1971 and later, are called 'Oil-in-Frame', 'Oil-Bearing' or 'Oilers' for short. However, BSA's brain trust never tested the new frames, and Triumph's engines wouldn't fit in the new frame on the assembly line. The rear rocker box needed to be removed, the engine installed, then the rocker box reinstalled, all on a moving assembly line.

New Oil-in-Frame Bonneville

The new Oiler 650s weren't warmly received in 1971, although they were handsome machines. Triumph had updated their looks considerably, bringing them closer to the mainstream while still retaining their British character and that 'Triumph' look. In 1973, they were punched out to 750cc, and the T120 became the T140 Bonneville, while the TR6 became the TR7. 1973 also brought a much-needed 5-speed gearbox and front disc brake. By this time, most of the Oilers' earlier problems had been sorted out, and they were becoming very nice bikes to ride, as long as you didn't press them too hard.

The 1983 Triumph T140W TSS was the last bike built by Triumph in the Meriden factory. It used a Westlake-developed 8-valve head and lots of other tricks to produce 58 horsepower at 6500rpm. Because of its forged crankshaft, it was also smoother than any Triumph twin before it. Another stunning achievement for the scrappy British. Unfortunately, it wasn't enough. Only 438 were built.

The Trident benefited from the new gear also, including all the new bodywork but not the oil-bearing frame. Then, in 1973, when the twins got 5 speeds and a disc brake, the Trident got them also. While all Triumph twin production was shut off for most of the 1974 model year, due to the Meriden worker takeover, Trident production had always been on the same line as the Rocket 3, in BSA's Small Heath factory, so Trident production, albeit small, continued unabated. Redesigned in its final year, 1975, it became the T160 Trident and had forward-leaning cylinders like the old Rocket 3, and at long last, an electric starter. It didn't help. Trident production ended in 1975. Total combined Trident and Rocket 3 production over its entire lifespan totalled about 27,000 bikes. By comparison, Honda built over 250,000 Goldwings in its first seven years of production.

The End Draws Near

As BSA imploded in 1972, it merged with Norton-Villiers, so Norton now owned Triumph. Norton wanted to close down Triumph's legendary Meriden plant and move Triumph production to Norton's factory at Donington Park. In 1974, the workers rebelled, blockading themselves in the factory, stopping any bikes from leaving. As a result, very few 1974 Bonnevilles or TR7s were built. Norton relented in 1975, allowing the workers to buy the company and form the Meriden Co-op. It never had enough capital to make the venture work and struggled along, producing fewer and fewer Bonnevilles every year (now the only model it produced), and some rather interesting 'specials', until it finally gave up the ghost in 1983. BSA built its last motorcycle in 1972, and the last Norton Commando rolled off the line in 1975. Triumph was the last one still standing. In 1983 the beleaguered co-op built the last Bonneville – almost.

Returned from the Grave

After the fall, a rich British developer bought what remained of the company and reintroduced the Triumph Motorcycle brand to the world in 1990 as a totally new, modern, high-performance bike, and the retro-styled Bonneville in 2001. These modern Triumphs are built in a state-of-the-art factory in Hinkley, England. Hence, all old-school bikes that were built in Triumph's old Meriden plant are called 'Meriden Triumphs', and the modern bikes are called 'Hinkley Triumphs'. The modern Bonneville is still a parallel twin, but now the crank pins are set at 270 degrees instead of 360, and they have DOHC and 4 valves per cylinder. The first Hinkley Bonneville in 2001 was an 800cc, but it's grown over the years to its present displacement of 1,200cc. Triumph also produces a wide range of mainstream bikes of every sort and is, today, a major force in the modern motorcycle industry.

This 2014 Triumph Bonneville has all the modern features: electronic fuel injection, DOHC w/8 valves, disc brakes, etc but still manages to retain the looks of a classic Bonneville. It started out at 800cc but has grown over the years to 1,200cc. The modern Triumph company makes a full line of world-class motorcycles today, almost single-handedly redeeming the reputation of British motorcycle manufacture.

Chapter 16
Velocette Motorcycles

In the Beginning
The early history of some of Britain's finest motorcycle manufacturers from the classic era are surprisingly similar. Velocette was established by a German-born émigré to England, just like Triumph. It started out making bicycles, just like Triumph, BSA, Matchless and Ariel. By 1896, Johannes Gutgemann was building bicycles, and in 1904 he bought out the Belgian firm Kelekom Motors and began experimenting with motorised bicycles. He'd changed his name to Taylor by this time, and his company Taylor, Gue Ltd produced its first true motorcycle in 1905, called the Veloce, with a whopping 2 horsepower. It failed miserably, and the company went broke. He changed names again, this time to John Goodman and formed a new company, Veloce Motors Ltd, to produce motorcycles.

The Early Years
After some early failures, by 1913 it launched a new 2-stroke motorcycle designed by Goodman's son Percy, who had now joined the company. They named the motorcycle 'Velocette'. It was the first use of the name, and by 1916 they had changed the name of the company to Velocette. World War One started, and all production was devoted to munitions for the duration. After the war, the new K1 250cc single did well in the marketplace and on the racetrack, including the Isle of Man TT. It pioneered several novel innovations for the time, like the throttle-controlled oil pump. It was also light, handled well and was powerful for its day. By 1930, Velocette had developed its new H-series 2-strokes, which it built until 1946.

This 1929 Velocette KTT brimmed with all the latest engine technologies, gleaned from Velocette's racing efforts. SOHC, shaft-driven with bevel gears on both ends, exposed hairpin valve springs and 9:1 compression helped to make these winning machines at the track.

Velocette K-Series

Velocette knew it needed to expand its product line to survive and so entered into the 4-stroke market in the early 1920s. The new machine was to be very advanced for the times, with an OHC, 350cc displacement and a single cylinder. It was introduced in 1925 as the 'K'-series (K for *kam*, the German word for cam). Soon the KTT was racing at the Isle of Man TT and Brooklands. The smooth-running, reliable machines scored very well in competition and cemented Velocette's reputation as a builder of high-quality motorcycles. Street versions were soon to follow including the KSS (Super Sports), KTP (twin-exhaust ports) and the KN (normal). The OHC engine continued on the roadsters until 1948, continuing to pioneer new innovations such as using strobe lights for accurate ignition timing, and the world's first positive-stop foot actuated gearchange.

1946 Velocette KSS. All K-series had OHC engines. Velocette built elegant-looking bikes that were also rugged and well-engineered.

M-Series

Velocette had great success with its OHC singles, but in 1933 it decided to introduce a new line of OHV (ie pushrods) machines, as a way of reducing its production costs while delivering a lower-priced motorcycle to market. The K-series had been expensive to produce. Skilled workers on the production line hand-assembled the tricky shaft-and-bevel camshaft drive. The simpler OHV design would be quicker to produce and would require much less highly skilled labour to assemble. The first of these was the Velocette MOV, a 250cc OHV single with a square bore-and-stroke ratio of 68mm x 68mm. It was an immediate hit and proved to be an able performer, capable of 78mph, a stunning speed at the time for a 250. MOVs were also known for their reliability and excellent handling.

The 350cc 1938 Velocette MAC was an OHV single, designed to be simpler and thus cheaper to produce than its bevel-drive OHC siblings, Velocette's K-series.

The MAC: Bigger is Better

The MOV was doing so well that a larger version was needed and by lengthening the stroke, the 350cc Velocette MAC was created in 1934. It became Velocette's best-selling model. The much-needed profits were invested in an entirely new design, a 500cc OHV single to be called the MSS in 1935. This utilised an all-new frame, developed from the Mk V KTT race machines and shared with the KSS Mk II, 1936–48. The MSS was another runaway hit for Velocette. Speaking of racing, Velocette took 1st, 2nd, 3rd and 4th places in the Juniors class (350cc) at the 1947 Isle of Man TT, and in 1950 it won the 350cc World Championship.

This ugly little mutant is a 1967 Velocette LE. At one time, Velocette thought it represented the future of motorcycling. Fortunately, for some strange reason, Britain's police forces loved them.

Post-War and the LE

Immediately following World War Two, there was a pressing need in the UK for simple, inexpensive, utilitarian personal transport to get to-and-from work. In 1948, Velocette attempted to tap into this market with their radical new 'LE'. It stood for 'Little Engine', and boy was it. The 149cc water-cooled, flathead horizontally opposed twin made all of 8 horsepower. It was mounted in an unsightly pressed-steel semi-step-through frame with a swing arm and telescopic forks. Designed by Charles Udall, it was supposed to be cheap and easy to produce, so that it could be delivered to the market at a very low price. However, the radical new design (including one of the earliest examples of unitised engine/transmission construction) proved to be complicated and expensive to produce. Strangely, despite all this, it proved to be a runaway bestseller for Velocette, in fact its best-selling model ever! Still, the high cost of tooling and manufacture made it almost impossible for Velocette to make a profit. One nice feather in its cap was the wholesale adoption of the LE by British Police.

The Velocette Vogue

Velocette entered the 1960s looking for direction. It thought it knew the way to go because the spartan LE had been such a good seller. It, therefore, introduced the odd Velocette Viceroy (a weird little 2-stroke scooter) in 1960, following it up just one year later in 1961 with the gorgeous, but misguided, Velocette Vogue. This fibreglass wonder was completely enclosed, offered decent rider protection, stowage and actually looked pretty good in the flesh. However, it still had only the same 8 horsepower as the LE with which it shared engines, but now it was even slower because of the added weight of the bodywork. It failed miserably and few were built.

This 1964 Velocette Vogue shows how elegant they were. Unfortunately, they were underpowered by 'The Little Engine that Couldn't'.

The Thruxton was the ultimate Velocette. Fast, light, good brakes and they handled well. This is a 1969 Velocette Thruxton.

High-Performance Velocettes

By the 1960s, the motorcycle market had clearly shifted away from practical, economical commuters, and towards high-performance bikes with sporting aspirations. Triumph, BSA and Norton were killing in this market, and by the mid-1960s, the Japanese were taking a major bite out of it for themselves. Velocette never developed a vertical twin like nearly all the other marques in Britain. Velocette had only big singles to work with, but it was very good at getting big power out of big singles, which was Velocette's specialty. First up was the 500 Venom. Then it reduced the bore, turning it into an incredibly robust 350: the Viper. Both came out in 1956. Vipers were very fast to begin with, but Velocette made all sorts of factory racing parts available to its customers, like close-ration gearboxes, racing magnetos, rear sets, alloy rims, etc. In 1961, a Velocette Venom became the first motorcycle in history to cover 2,400 miles in 24 hours. The ultimate evolution of the line was the 500 Thruxton, much faster than the Venom, with 10:1 compression, a hotter cam and an Amal TT carburettor. A Thruxton won the Isle of Mann TT in 1967. Despite all this, Velocette was fighting to survive, financially.

The Indian Connection

American motorcycle maker Indian had struggled for most of its life. By 1953, Indian was DOA and passed through several hands, all of whom had their own ideas of what an Indian motorcycle should look like. Interestingly, from 1953 until 1971, every Indian motorcycle built was either British-influenced, British-built or had a British engine. In 1963, motorcycle repair manual giant Floyd Clymer bought the Indian brand and in 1967 began producing Indian motorcycles in Italy with Royal Enfield 750 twin engines.

They were well-made bikes with top-quality components but too expensive to sell well. Clymer tried the same thing using Velocette 500 Venom engines in 1969 calling the new bike the

'Repair Manual King' Floyd Clymer dropped a Velocette engine into an Italian frame to create the 1970 Indian Velo 500. Only 122 were built.

Indian Velo 500. It too failed after just 122 were produced. In 1970, both Royal Enfield and Velocette went out of business, ending Clymer's supply of engines. Then in the same year, Clymer himself died, and that was the end of the venture.

The End

Alas, nothing could save Velocette. Its products were hopelessly outclassed and made obsolete by the onslaught of modern, reliable bikes from Japan. It was undercapitalised and so had no hope of developing a new line of state-of-the-art machines. It was still deeply ensconced in old-world design and manufacturing processes, which were craftsman intensive and produced low volumes of products. Like so many classic British motorcycle manufacturers, Velocette was a dinosaur in an increasingly modern world, and in 1970 it became extinct.

Chapter 17

Vincent Motorcycles

Larger than Life

Vincent Motorcycles has an aura and a cache to it that vastly outweighs its production numbers. From the end of World War Two until Vincent closed its doors in 1955, it produced fewer than 11,000 units in total, yet its image and reputation among the British motorcycle faithful is larger than life. At classic motorcycle shows Vincents draw crowds. At auction, they often bring six-figure sums. In a way, Vincents have taken on a status much like old Ferraris or Rolls-Royces, which were also produced in very low numbers, yet command respect, admiration and high auction prices. Vincent's premier bike, the Black Shadow, was certainly a beautiful piece of machinery with its gloss black engine, but it was also extremely fast in its day, having earned the title 'The World's Fastest Motorcycle'.

Like all Vincents, the 1938 Vincent Rapide oozed with quality. They were the Rolls-Royce of motorcycles in their day.

This 1954 Vincent Rapide 998cc V-twin gives a good view of its cantilever rear suspension. The triangulated rear section pivots on a low axis just behind the gearbox, with the spring-loaded twin shocks semi-horizontal under the seat. It didn't provide much travel and flexed a lot, but in a day when most bikes had rigid frames, it was considered 'advanced'.

Vincent's Early Days

The Vincent story begins in World War One, when young British RAF pilot Howard Raymond Davis was shot down and captured by the Germans in 1917. While a POW, he conceived a motorcycle design that he planned to produce after the war. The resulting company, HRD (Davis's initials) built motorcycles using JAP engines until 1928, when it went broke. Along came Phil Vincent, flush with cash from the Argentine cattle business. He bought HRD out of receivership for a mere £450. He renamed the company Vincent-HRD. It started out building motorcycles with engines purchased elsewhere. In 1934, it began producing its own engines. Vincents were always well designed, well built and unique. At a time when most bikes used rigid frames, the Vincent used a set-up similar in many ways to Harley's Softail, called the 'cantilever' frame. The entire rear section of the bike pivoted on a swing arm with the shocks mounted horizontally under the seat. It looked like a conventional rigid frame at first glance but offered some much-needed suspension travel. Another unique feature was the two valve guides on each valve, one high and one low with a forked rocker arm in between. It was meant to prolong valve guide life, and it worked.

Wartime Blues

World War Two saw Vincent making munitions and marine engines but not motorcycles. At the war's end, Phil Vincent set about opening up the US market. However, Harley-Davidson, H-D for short, objected to Vincent using the HRD name in America, claiming it would create confusion in the marketplace, so the 'HRD' part was dropped, and from then on, they were simply called 'Vincents'. Its biggest sellers at the time were 500cc singles, the Meteor and the Comet, good for around 26 horsepower and a 90mph top speed. However, even before the war, Vincent knew it needed much more power if it wanted to compete in the burgeoning US motorcycle market. How could the low-volume, cash-strapped Vincent come up with a new motorcycle with twice the power? That's an interesting story.

Presto! From a single to a twin. Vincent kept it simple by just doubling the existing Comet single (left), turning it into a V-twin, like this Rapide engine (right).

Funny Story…

Prior to the war, Phil Irving, Vincent's chief engineer, was sitting at the drawing board with two tracings of the Vincent 499cc single-cylinder engine. As things got moved around, the top tracing roughly lined up with the bottom one at an angle that made it look like a V-twin. With a little cajoling, he lined it all up and the Vincent V-twin was born. The new 998cc 1936 Series A Rapide made 45 horsepower and was good for 110mph, stellar at the time. It was produced in low numbers until civilian production was curtailed by World War Two in 1939. After the war, it was completely redesigned and the resulting 1946 Series B Rapide was a monster. They put two front brakes on it to counter the added speed. The Series C came out in 1948, with Girling's new Girdraulic forks instead of the old Brampton girders. However, the big news was the addition of a new high-performance version dubbed the Black Shadow, now making 55 horsepower and topping out at 125mph, hence the title 'The World's Fastest Production Motorcycle'. Black Shadows are famous for their gloss black engines. Rapide engines were finished in polished aluminium.

The 499cc Comet was Vincent's biggest seller by far. Literally half of a Rapide V-twin, the Comet used the same sophisticated chassis, suspension and brakes as its bigger brother. This is a 1950 Vincent Comet Series C.

The top-dog Vincent was the 998cc Black Shadow V-twin. Note the similarities with the Comet, above. This is a 1952 Series C Black Shadow.

The Bathing Suit Bike

They weren't kidding about being the 'World's Fastest Motorcycle'. On 13 September 1948, Rolland 'Rollie' Free piloted his modified Vincent Black Lightning into the history books at the Bonneville Salt Flats. At the time, the 150mph barrier seemed unreachable for motorcycles. Rollie tried several times, but never quite touched the 'Big 150'. He determined that it was the wind resistance of his clothing that was slowing him down, so he stripped down to a bathing suit, a bathing cap and a pair of borrowed sneakers, then removed the seat and lay prone on the back fender. His 2-way average jumped to 150.313mph. The picture of him breaking the record is one of the most iconic photos in the motorcycle world. The record-breaking Black Lightning forever became known as the 'Bathing Suit Bike'. It is still around today, fully restored and making the show circuit.

This is why they call it the 'Bathing Suit Bike'.

This is what the Bathing Suit Bike looks like today, fully restored.

Crazy Ideas that Failed Anyway

Despite their success on the Salt, Vincent struggled financially. Phil Vincent tried many different, and sometimes crazy, things to turn it around. Motorcycles with fully enclosed bodies were an expensive experiment that failed to catch on. Then Vincent tried a trike with a 998cc Rapide V-twin capable of 117mph. It too bombed in the market. Next it became the importer of NSU mopeds, selling more than 20,000 NSU Quickly mopeds in 1954 alone, so good in fact that NSU pulled its contract and began importing them itself. In 1955 Phil Vincent finally pulled the plug, ending a brilliant career in motorcycle production. He vowed, however, that Vincent parts would always be available, and in fact they still are today. A testament to the solidity of Vincent the motorcycle and Vincent the man.

This amorphous blob is a 1955 Vincent Black Knight. In England, where riders routinely dealt with bad weather, it was meant to offer some comfort, and be easier to wipe down at the end of the day. Alas, it was a concept before its time.

A New Lease of Life

Swiss racer/engineer Fritz Egli designed and built custom frame kits for the legendary Vincent 998cc V-twin engine, known for their perfect welding beads and luscious nickel-plating. He built around 100 frames from 1967 to 1972, with the intent of modernising the iconic Vincent Black Shadow, which fell out of production in 1955. Each frame was hand-built to a high standard, most were custom-built to customers' specifications, so that nearly every genuine Egli that you see is different. Egli-Vincents are very much like the original Shelby Cobra of the 1960s. Only around 1,000 Cobras were built, but today an estimated 30,000 replicas ply the streets. They were so popular yet so rare, that an entire industry sprang up to copy the Cobra's good looks. The same thing has happened with the Egli-Vincent. Today, and for many years now, frame-builders have been copying Egli frames, and it's hard to tell them apart from the originals.

Fritz Egli built modern frames around Vincent V-twins in the 1960s and 1970s. This is a 1970 Egli-Vincent cafe racer. Original Egli-Vincents are worth big money today.

PART 3: THE BITTER END AND BEYOND

Chapter 18

The Death of the British Motorcycle Industry

Many factors contributed to the demise of the British motorcycle industry. Many of them were the same factors that conspired to crush the British automotive industry as well at about the same time.

Times were a-changing, and the British seemed unwilling, or unable, to stay ahead of the wave. After a long run as the world's premier manufacturers, new players (primarily from Japan) employing modern methods, were eating their lunch. Lacking the will was one problem, but a lack of the means to do what needed to be done was an even bigger problem. Where Japanese companies were getting strategic and financial help from the Japanese government, which was trying to build up its economy, the British government scorned its businesses, provided no help or protection and left them to fend for themselves. By the 1980s, Britain, once the proud maker of some of the world's greatest sports cars and motorcycles, had ceased nearly all production. Very little remained and what did was snapped up by foreign companies.

Today, Jaguar and Land Rover are owned by Tata Motors (India), Rolls-Royce and Mini are owned by BMW (Germany), Bentley is owned by Volkswagen (Germany), and even tiny Lotus is owned by Proton (China). The only independent carmakers in Britain today are Morgan (very old) and McLaren (very new), both of which are tiny in terms of production numbers. Royal Enfield is owned by Madras Motors of India, and BSA is now owned by Indian tractor giant Mahindra.

However, government neglect was just part of the problem. There must have been something in the psyche of these great men of industry that forced them to stubbornly hold on to their old methods and ideas. Edward Turner, who designed both the first Ariel Square Four, then the seminal Triumph parallel twin, became the master of Triumph design for decades. He was so in love with his original 1938 design of the parallel twin that he refused to consider any alternatives. He even visited Japan in 1960 and came back

After years of building only lightweight bikes, Honda fired a shot across Britain's bow with the 1965 Honda CB450, affectionately known as the 'Black Bomber'. It outclassed the British 650 twins in almost every way, and this was only the beginning, as more, bigger and better motorcycles came pouring out of Japan.

with the belief that the Japanese were backward, posed no serious competition and that the British were on the right course. That's arrogance.

The antiquated designs of the bikes themselves were part of the problem. Pushrods, drum brakes, 4 speeds, oil leaks, vibration and sketchy reliability couldn't trump the modern all-alloy OHC and DOHC engines, 5 speeds, disc brakes and smooth, trouble-free operation of the bikes coming out of Japan, and all for a lower price. However, the manufacturing methods used to produce the bikes were just as backward. Meanwhile, over in Japan, huge state-of-the-art factories were churning out bikes by the thousands.

By the mid-1960s, Honda alone was producing more bikes in a month than the entire British motorcycle industry built in a year. In 1968, Honda, a fairly young company compared to the ancient British firms, built its ten millionth motorcycle. How can you compete with that?

In addition to all this other heavy baggage, the British manufacturers were saddled with bad management, greed, arrogance and hubris. BSA, always at the centre of the British motorcycle industry and the only one strong enough to take the lead, exited the 1950s a true industrial giant riding on a wave of success. Unfortunately, the deal that brought Triumph and Ariel under BSA's wing, also

The British actually beat the 1969 Honda CB750 Four to market by several weeks in 1968 with their own multi-cylinder superbikes, the Triumph Trident and the BSA Rocket 3. However, when the mighty Honda hit the ground, it was game over for the British manufacturers. Life would never be the same for the British motorcycle industry.

At a time when BSA's and Triumph's product lines were in sore need of modernisation, or new engines, or better electrics to compete with the Japanese, instead, they bought this lavish country estate called Umberslade Hall to serve as their new design centre. However, very little of use came from it, such as a 350 twin that never reached production, and the 1971 oil-bearing frames that wouldn't allow the engines to be installed in one piece on the production line. What they did accomplish could have been done just as well from a modest shop.

brought with it Jack Sangster, who garnered himself a seat on BSA's board. In a little less than ten years, he took this once mighty industrial giant down to a hollowed-out shell of its former self, having sold off all the assets and lost most of the good people. This left BSA entering the turbulent 1960s on shaky footing and thus unable to endure the crushing competition from Japan.

It was the old versus the new. Europe's age-old artisan culture versus modern, high-tech Japan. What a matchup. The outcome was inevitable, and the British motorcycle industry, just like the British automotive industry, quickly fell apart.

However, the industry overall was weak even before the Japanese arrived. Vincent closed in 1955; Ariel wasn't far behind. By 1960, AMC was barely selling enough Matchless and AJS singles, once its bestsellers, to justify production, and by 1966, the once mighty conglomerate went belly up. Only the Norton Commando survived. Royal Enfield (the British one) and Velocette stopped building bikes in 1967. By 1972, BSA was done. The gorgeous Commando only made it to 1975, and after a complete redesign, even the Triumph Trident was discontinued after only one year, in 1975. This left only the Triumph Bonneville.

Prior to BSA's collapse in 1972, a merger was attempted between Triumph, BSA and Norton to hopefully gain enough strength to survive. It didn't work; BSA closed its doors anyway. This left Triumph in the hands of Norton, which decided to close Triumph's famous factory in Meriden and move Triumph production over to its own factory at Donington Park to cut costs. At the start of the 1974 model year, the Triumph workers responded by barricading themselves in the factory and not letting anything in or out. It took until nearly the end of the 1974 model year (hence there are very few 1974 Bonnevilles) for Norton to capitulate and allow the workers to form their own worker-owned co-op, called the Meriden Co-op, and to buy the company.

Triumph hit the ground running in 1975, but was undercapitalised from the start and struggled just to keep the lights on. Each subsequent year was worse than the last. The value of the British pound to the US dollar made its motorcycles more expensive, whereas Japan's bikes enjoyed the opposite effect. Sales continued to lag and production suffered. Trident production had continued through the strike because they had always been built at BSA's old Small Heath factory, on the same line as the BSA Rocket 3s. Even this ran out by 1975. However, the clever workers in Meriden found low-cost ways of making improvements to their bikes, including changing over to

Despite the strike, and with almost no money to work with, the scrappy lads at Triumph managed to completely re-engineer the T150 Trident into the 1975 Triumph T160 Trident. It then had a first ever electric starter and was converted over to left-foot-shifting, in addition to being completely restyled. It lasted one year only. There was no 1976 Trident.

Triumph spun several 'special editions' off of the evergreen Bonneville including the 1977 T140J Silver Jubilee, cashing in on the big 25th anniversary celebration of the Queen's coronation. This one is a US-spec model with the teardrop tank. The UK-spec version came with a square tank. Other specials followed, including the 1981 T140LE 'Royal Wedding' Edition, celebrating the wedding of Prince Charles and Lady Diana Spencer.

A plaque at the former site of Triumph's legendary Meriden factory. Opened in 1942, after its former factory was bombed by the Germans in 1940, it remained in operation until the collapse of the Meriden Co-op in 1983.

left-foot-shifting when mandated by the US government in 1975. They also created several rather interesting 'specials', all based on the venerable Bonneville.

Alas, it couldn't possibly last the way it was going. Triumph often wasn't able to pay suppliers, who then stopped shipping it the parts needed to build its bikes. Many of its British suppliers dropped the company, forcing it to buy its tanks, controls, switchgear and so forth from Italy. Even this was only a temporary measure. By 1983, it could go no further. The wolves were at the door and it slipped into receivership. The lights went out for the last time at the Meriden factory on 26 August and that was the end of the story of the classic British motorcycle – almost.

Chapter 19
Life After Death

When the Meriden Co-op slipped into receivership, British billionaire real estate developer John Bloor bought the entire company for around $200,000. This included the brand name, the tooling, the designs and all the leftover parts. He planned to reopen quickly with a modernised line of Triumph's classic bikes. This proved to be a bigger task than he bargained for, forcing him to change his plans to building modern bikes. However, it would take a few years to put everything in motion.

Triumph at this point (1983) had the distinction of being the oldest continually operating motorcycle manufacturer in the world, having started production in 1902. Bloor didn't want to lose that title. So, he licensed the rights and the tooling for the Bonneville to Les Harris, who hand-built them in small numbers in England until 1990 when Bloor was ready to open the new Triumph company.

The rest is history. Triumph started producing world-class, state-of-the-art 3- and 4-cylinder bikes and just expanded out from there. By 2000, it introduced a retro-styled, but totally modern, Bonneville with 800cc DOHC, 4-valves-per-cylinder and a level of quality that rivalled the best bikes built anywhere, including Japan.

Around 2000, the world slipped into the early stages of a retro boom. The auto industry quickly followed, with the Volkswagen New Beetle, the Dodge Viper, the 2002-05 Ford Thunderbird, the 2005 Mustang, and the new Camaro and Challenger. Suddenly old was in.

Royal Enfield Bullets (500 singles) were still being produced in India and looked almost the same as they did in the 1950s. Russian-made Ural motorcycles that looked like they were built during World War Two were suddenly in style in the US and Europe. The first Norton 961 Commandos were rolling out around this same time, and while totally modern, they had a distinct retro presence.

Then in 2016, Mahindra, the world's largest tractor manufacturer, bought the rights to the BSA name, and everyone had high hopes for a new line of BSAs. Mahindra certainly had the resources, financial, technical and industrial, to pull it off. The first of the new Mahindra-BSAs were supposed to launch in 2019, but it hasn't happened yet. Everyone is hopeful.

When Triumph closed in 1983, it was bought out of receivership by John Bloor. He licensed the rights to the Bonneville to Les Harris, who practically hand-built Bonnevilles from 1983 until the new Triumph brand could be kick-started in 1990. This allowed Triumph to claim to be the oldest continuously operating motorcycle company in the world, having started in 1902. Les Harris built a fine machine.

Just like with cars, classic motorcycle brands with good reputations are making a comeback, always under new ownership, with new ideas. It just goes to show how endearing these wonderful old machines were and are today and the impact they had on individual lives and society as a whole. There are many lessons to learn from the rise and fall of the British motorcycle industry. America is going through very much the same thing today, except with China this time, not Japan.

Just like in the past, in modern times, the British have shown the world that they can build a truly world-class motorcycle that can compete with the best from Europe and Japan. Again, Triumph is leading the way, but others like Norton contribute with great design flare and engineering prowess, albeit at low production volumes. The British motorcycle industry isn't what it used to be, but the world isn't what it used to be, either. The British are probably better equipped today to compete in the modern marketplace than at any other time in their history. Of this, and of their illustrious past, they should be proud.

This 2009 Triumph Bonneville Thruxton has a serious retro-vibe, but Triumph also builds contemporary bikes of nearly every shape and size.

Norton is building motorcycles again, at a rate of 1,000 to 2,000 per year. While this 2010 Norton 961 Commando is a thoroughly modern sport bike, it is also instantly recognisable as a Norton.

Picture Credits

Page 5: Meriden.triumph; https://creativecommons.org/licenses/by-sa/4.0/legalcode
Page 6: Forbes, Archibald, *Battles of the Nineteenth Century*, Cassell and Company (1901)
Page 7, left: Yesterdays Antique Motorcycles; https://creativecommons.org/licenses/by-sa/4.0/legalcode
Page 7, right: public domain.
Page 8, top: with permission from Ron Glenister.
Page 8, bottom: sv1ambo; https://creativecommons.org/licenses/by/2.0/legalcode
Page 9: public domain.
Page 10: with permission from Jane Concha.
Page 11, top: Daniel Hartwig; https://creativecommons.org/licenses/by/2.0/legalcode
Page 11, bottom left: Daniel Hartwig; https://creativecommons.org/licenses/by/2.0/legalcode
Page 11, bottom right: Thomas's Pics; https://creativecommons.org/licenses/by/2.0/legalcode
Page 12: Lissák Tivadar; https://creativecommons.org/licenses/by-sa/3.0/legalcode
Page 18: Alf van Beem; https://creativecommons.org/publicdomain/zero/1.0/legalcode
Page 19, top: SG2012; https://creativecommons.org/licenses/by/2.0/legalcode
Page 22: with permission from Chris Lawson.
Page 25, top: with permission from Fred Marsch.
Page 26: Khaosaming; https://creativecommons.org/licenses/by-sa/3.0/legalcode
Page 29, bottom: Rama; https://creativecommons.org/licenses/by-sa/2.0/fr/legalcode
Page 32: SG2012; https://creativecommons.org/licenses/by/2.0/legalcode
Page 39, bottom: Yesterdays Antique Motorcycles; https://creativecommons.org/licenses/by-sa/4.0/legalcode
Page 43: SG2012; https://creativecommons.org/licenses/by/2.0/legalcode
Page 46: Yesterdays Antique Motorcycles; https://creativecommons.org/licenses/by-sa/4.0/legalcode
Page 48: Ronald Saunders; https://creativecommons.org/licenses/by-sa/2.0/legalcode
Page 53, top: State Library of New South Wales collections.
Page 54, top: Thruxton; https://creativecommons.org/licenses/by/3.0/deed.en
Page 64, bottom: Yesterdays Antique Motorcycles; https://creativecommons.org/licenses/by-sa/4.0/legalcode
Page 66: Bob Adams; https://creativecommons.org/licenses/by-sa/2.0/legalcode
Page 68: AxelKing; https://creativecommons.org/licenses/by-sa/3.0/de/legalcode
Page 82, top: Mick; https://creativecommons.org/licenses/by/2.0/legalcode
Page 88, top: trademark of Harris Vincent Gallery, Inc.
Page 91, bottom: Philip Halling; https://creativecommons.org/licenses/by-sa/2.0/legalcode
Page 93, bottom: Amanda Slater; https://creativecommons.org/licenses/by-sa/2.0/legalcode
Page 94: public domain.